PEAR FLAT PHILOSOPHIES

PEAR FLAT PHILOSOPHIES

by

Larry L. Weishuhn

SAFARI PRESS, INC.
P.O. Box 3095, Long Beach, CA 90803,
USA

Weishuhn, Larry L.

Second Edition

ISBN 0-940143-85-2

1993, Long Beach, California

10 9 8 7 6 5 4 3 2

Readers wishing to receive the Safari Press catalog, featuring many
fine books on big-game hunting, wingshooting, and firearms,
should write the publisher at the address given above.

42nd title published by Safari Press

Table of Contents

FOREWORD

Hunting, whether for gray squirrels in some deep hard-wood hollow in Alabama or for Dall sheep on a barren, craggy mountaintop in Alaska, is an adventure that is meant to be shared. We hunters are very selective when it comes to selecting the right person to be our hunting buddy.

He must possess special traits if we are to "drink from the same cup." We want our hunting buddy to have the skills of an Indian guide. It's comforting to know he has a working knowledge in subjects such as camping, navigation, tracking, survival, gunsmithing, reloading, and outdoor cooking. Since we will spend many long, hard days in the field and cold nights in camp, we want our hunting buddy to be always cheerful and positive. He should have the strength of a pack mule so he can help drag our buck back to camp, cut great stacks of firewood, and haul gallons of water from some distant spring. Perhaps most importantly, he must have the skills of a good storyteller, for after the hunt is over, it is the stories that let us relive those adventures over and over again.

I am one of the lucky hunters, for I have found the perfect hunting buddy. Larry Weishuhn possesses all of the traits we normally look for in a hunting buddy, plus many more. Aside from being a master outdoorsman, hunter, and marksman, Larry is a white-tailed deer biologist who is sought out by other biologists when they have a question about deer management. He has the disposition of a saint. I have seen him smile and joke as he single-handedly prepared a meal for eight hungry hunters, bring in wood for the campfire, and skin three deer in the rain, all of this after having not slept for more than two hours in two days. His sense of humor makes the worst of conditions simply funny. I have seen him laugh when the truck we depended upon to get back to civilization was lying on its side in a mud-filled gully. Bitter cold days, leaky tents, wet firewood, soggy food, and unplanned nights spent on a rock ledge without a sleeping bag are not hardships to Larry, but only the makings of great stories to be told in future camps.

For years my wife and I have been among the few who had the privilege of sitting around a campfire in some remote hunting camp watching the twinkle in Larry's eyes when he would look into the fire, push back his beat-up old Stetson, and with a grin, begin with, "I'll never forget the time when. . . ." I knew I was going to share another great adventure with a great adventurer. Now, thanks to this book, you, too, can have Larry as your hunting buddy. Through his unique story-telling ability, you can share some of his hunting adventures. So kick off your boots, freshen up your branch water, throw another log on the fire, and listen to Larry as he tells you some of his *Pear Flat Philosophies*. It's the next best thing to being there.

J. Wayne Fears
Cross Creek Hollow, Alabama
January 21, 1993

Dedication

To my wife, Mary Anne, and daughters, Theresa and Beth, who have shared my life, even when I was absent from home. To my parents, Lester and Lillie Weishuhn, who early in life instilled in me a love for the out-of-doors and hunting. To the many "characters" with whom it has been my pleasure to have shared past campfires, and such is most definitely the case here! While my desire to write a book is apparently innate, had it not been for the questioning and encouragement of hunting partners such as Ron Porter, J. Wayne and Sherry Fears, and others, this volume of words would likely never have been seen to completion.

Some of the various "chapters" in loose form have been seen under my "View From the Pear Flat" column, which appears regularly in the *UVALDE LEADER NEWS* and *SOUTH-ERN LIVESTOCK STANDARD*. I am appreciative of those publications, their editors, publishers, and staff for allowing me the use of some of those basic columns. "Jubel, The Lonesome Dove Turkey" appeared in somewhat similar form in *THE TURKEY HUNTER*. My thanks for allowing me to use it in this book. The two chapters concerning horn rattling contain happenings that have been written and spoken about, most notably in *NORTH AMERICAN HUNTER*. My thanks to Bill Miller, Mark LaBarbera, and their staff.

I am especially appreciative of the many individuals named in the text, for this is truly their book. Their names follow in the various chapters. But some others must be named here as well: friends such as Herbert Aschenbeck, E.V. and Laura Belle Potter, Dr. R.M. Robinson, David O'Keeffe, Bret Triplett, Jerry Baker, Jerry Johnston, Richard Petrini, Jay Verzuh, Marcia Porter,

Anthony Ellis, Gary Machen, Murphy Ray, Homer Saye, Hal Swiggett, Craig Boddington, John Wootters, Jay Gates, Gordon Whittington, Bill Buckley, Jerry Smith, Max and Carolyn Williams, and the many other fellow hunters, guides, and outfitters with whom I have shared late-night campfires and sessions!

Thanks to my wife, Mary Anne, for putting up with my early-morning risings and writing sessions and for critiquing the manuscript even when sometimes it seemed as though I didn't appreciate it. Special thanks to Sherry K. Fears for her help with editing the manuscript and for her constructive comments. A very dear thank you and acknowledgement to Don Keller, an old friend and artist, whose drawings illustrate this book.

Lessons of a Grandfather

The last of the campfire's flames were casting long, indistinct shadows against the log cabin's walls, secreted in Cross Creek Hollow. I poked at the coals and sent a spray of glowing sparks skyward. They seemed momentarily to mingle with the stars above, before disappearing like shooting stars into the depths of endless inky-black night. The coolness of the December night, the fading embers shared with an old friend, and the long hours in the field matching wits with whitetails brought on a reflective mood. The black, gray, and flickering orange and yellow hues of what was left of the coals seemed to mesmerize both Wayne Fears and me. We sat silently across the fire pit, each lost in thought.

Earlier the discussion had been of great stags hunted, mountains climbed, and fine guns shot. The talk had brought back many memories of hunting as a youngster, hunting with my dad and maternal granddad. I tried to recall my first hunting or fishing trip. Such an occasion should be a highlight in anyone's life, but try as I might, those first experiences afield were lost deep within the recesses of gray matter, now crowded with many other days afield. Perhaps the reason those early days escaped my memory was I started hunting with my dad and fishing with my granddad long before I grew out of diapers. By the time I started forming words and thus making memories, I had already been instilled with a love of hunting, fishing, and the out-of-doors. As Red Ryder and Daisy BB guns replaced Roy Rogers cap pistols and as cane poles with cork bobbers became near constant companions, I was taught to respect what I hunted and fished.

There were times when my grandfather was the most important man in the world. He had patience and understanding to teach a considerably less patient grandson. The lessons he taught were of life, and how even the seemingly least important factor or item can and does play a major role in the scheme of nature. In his own way he explained nature to me. He showed me once how one small minnow might seem insignificant to some people, but, for the perpetuation of species in the chain above the minnow, then that minnow was mighty important. The lessons he taught about the survival of the animals, fish, and fowl in our environment was to become my most deep-seated memories.

Like many youngsters, I was fascinated by tadpoles and mosquito "wiggletails" found in small pools after a spring rain. Some of each of these species would provide food for larger creatures, yet Nature always made sure others survived to reach maturity and reproduce, starting the entire cycle over and over again. Once the adults had accomplished their purposes in life they returned to the Earth, passing their nutrients on to the soil to be utilized by ensuing and suc-ceeding generations of plants and animals.

In his own way he taught me not only of life, but of death as well. In this world, practically all life depends upon the death of other organisms. It is simply Nature's way, a rule that cannot be changed, broached, or rerouted. Life is con-tinually recycled. Nothing truly ever dies, it simply exists in different forms. I was to remember those early lessons when, as a third-grader, I learned my grandfather had passed away. Now, as I watched the sparks from the campfire, I was again reminded of his lessons, which in turn brought his presence closer to me. My grandfather's love of nature, which he passed on to me, has been his greatest legacy—a legacy that renews itself each year and a legacy that keeps my grandfather close. In some respects, my granddad has never left my side.

Staring into the coals, I recalled a scene many years ago when, without permission, I had used my grandfather's "tobaccy" knife to dig marble holes. The old man looked down his nose at his freckle-faced grandson. My face must have been the color of the red bandanna I wore around my neck. I knew I had done wrong, even if digging marble holes cleaned the knife of the accumulation left by many cuttings of Brown Mule. I held the knife at arm's length. Fear gripped every muscle

LESSONS OF A GRANDFATHER

and nerve in my five-year-old body. The old man reached for the knife and took it from my trembling hand, which was seemingly keeping time with my trembling lower lip. He carefully examined his Old Timer and put the knife in his pocket, without saying a word. When he motioned me to go out behind the woodshed, tears started welling up in my eyes. I knew I had done wrong, had 'fessed up to it, and would now have to pay the consequences, no matter how dire they might be. The thought of a million promises would not forestall the inevitable.

The old man spoke, "Do you now know better than to take someone's knife without first asking permission?"

I responded with a meek, "Yessir."

"Well, then perhaps you better go to the house and get my .22 rifle and bring along your BB gun. Maybe the two of us can find a couple of squirrels for supper. Grandma's squirrel stew sure would taste good this evening. Besides, I think it's about time you learned how to skin a squirrel."

Across the fire my compadre announced he was turning in, tomorrow would bring more white-tailed deer hunting adventures, and he wanted to be ready for the moment—if the morrow indeed was "the day." I told him that I would soon follow, but that I wanted to enjoy the peace and solitude of the dying fire. Somewhere off in the distance could be heard the sounds of a great horned owl, which likely brought terror to the hearts of the lesser night creatures. Even farther in the distance could be heard the lonesome, yet adventurous shrill of a train whistle. It sounded not unlike the train whistle that we could hear at my granddad's house, when conditions were just right. Those just-right conditions usually meant late fall or winter when there were few leaves on the trees to absorb the sound, coupled with a slight breeze blowing out of the northeast and bringing with it the sharpness of cool weather. The whistle of a train reminded me of nights spent talking about squirrel hunting, and how in my grandfather's youth, squirrels often provided more than hunting days afield—they provided meals for the local residents who might have otherwise gone to bed hungry.

When the pecan trees in the bottoms started dropping their delicious mast, the squirrels were at their best. Like the mailman of years gone by, neither rain, sleet, snow, nor the dark of night, to say nothing of mad dogs, could keep the mailman from his appointed rounds. The same could be said about my grandfather and me when it came to hunting squirrels. Adverse weather had little effect on our hunting activities, and the dark of night was occupied by hunting raccoons with my dad and his 'coon hounds.

Packing a pair of single-shot .22s, and being lead to the tall tree bottoms by his old dog, Hunter, the three of us put many a squirrel up a tree. The old liver and white pointer, turned squirrel dog, was an ace at his job. When he "put" a squirrel up a tree, he barked "treed" and waited patiently for my grandfather and me to appear on the scene. When we did, ol' Hunter circled the tree. The squirrel, in his efforts to keep the tree between himself and the animal making the noise, scrambled to our side of the tree. When he did, the old man's .22 made sort of a "pwhap" sound. The squirrel tumbled to the ground, neatly taken with a head shot.

After praising Hunter for his work, we moved on through the bottom and repeated the process until we had four or five squirrels, just enough to make a meal for my grandfather, grandmother, and me. Only on rare occasions when there was a big squirrel stew planned for more than the three of us, did we shoot any more. "Always leave a few for seed, never take more than what you need," he'd remind me when I prodded him to hunt longer.

These days all too often the joys of squirrel hunting are forgotten, or at best overlooked, and unfortunately the art of skinning and cleaning squirrels has been lost. In my youth, my granddad, dad, uncles, and even my grandmother and mother could skin and clean a squirrel without so much as leaving one hair on the carcass. Once we had skinned and cleaned our harvest of pecan eaters, my grandmother could turn them into dishes that could have been served to the most delicate of palates and have them asking for more.

During the nine years I shared with my grandfather, he had a tremendous influence upon my life, which in turn helped shape my future. His lessons were much farther-reaching than a young lad more interested in fishing for perch in the creek or hunting squirrels realized. In teaching me to hunt and then

LESSONS OF A GRANDFATHER

skin and clean squirrels, he taught me many valuable lessons about life and the workings of Nature. He taught me the value of a good dog, how to use a gun, the importance of telling the truth, and how to tell and appreciate a good tale. As we skinned a squirrel, he talked of his past experiences. Whenever I was too quick with the skinning detail, he slowed me down.

"Patience is not just a virtue (he never spoke down to me, even when I was extremely small), it's just plain old common sense. When you get in a rush, you make mistakes. If you get into a big hurry skinning a squirrel, you get hair all over the meat and you have to spend extra time picking it off. If you take your time and do it right the first time, you'll end up with a squirrel ready for the pot."

The damp cold of the night, now grown colder without the warmth of a fire, long since died from lack of fuel, brought me back to the present. Making sure the fire could under no circumstances again blaze, I headed toward the cabin. I pulled off my boots at the door and hung the old wool coat on a deer horn, just inside the door. In heading through the darkness toward my bed, I stumbled into the old rocking chair sitting in front of the potbellied stove. The audible "clunk" of my bare toe striking the hard oak, followed by a loud hissing sound as I drew in a quick deep breath of air to cope with the pain brought a stir from Mistah Fears' side of the room. The creak of the old bed was followed by a query addressing my health and well-being. Sinking slowly to my bed, I grunted a response, sat in thought for a few moments, then spoke. "Mistah Fears, what was the most valuable lesson your grandfather ever taught you?"

The query was followed by noticeable silence as the one questioned gathered his thoughts clouded by the sleep from which I had roused him. The old pine-slab bed on his side of the room creaked several times as he sat up. My companion took a deep breath, hesitated, then spoke. "Why, I guess the most important lesson he ever taught me was how to skin a squirrel. . . ."

Anticipating a renewed discussion, I stood up, limped over toward the potbellied stove, opened the door, and shoved in a piece of split oak. As I did, I remembered another lesson my grandfather taught me many years ago, "In some hunting camps it doesn't take long to spend a night!"

Reflections On A First Deer

Most people's lives are filled with firsts—first day at school, first date, first kiss, first car—but for me perhaps none of my firsts was more important than my first whitetail. Growing up in rural Texas when the white-tailed deer populations were just starting to rebound from such things as hungry citizens, prolonged drought, and screwworms was an exciting time for a youngster who lived, breathed, and dreamed hunting. Work and school were a way of life, interrupted by the latest issues of various outdoor journals. Wages earned from shucking corn, hauling hay, and the like were spent primarily to keep my single shot .22 stocked with sufficient squirrel and rabbit fodder and to pay for outdoor magazine subscriptions.

Hunting was a way of life for me and my family, and the only diversion we had from chores. Since the people in my community prized white-tailed deer and since I had started hunting while I was still in diapers, it was only natural for me to dream of taking my first white-tailed buck. Back then when I was growing up in the 1950s, a boy was considered a man when he did a day's work and when he took his first white-tailed buck. I knew full well that I could handle the first part; it was the second part that gave me trouble.

With each new issue of the hunting magazines I subscribed to came dreams of stalking big game with the experts. I literally hung on every word written by Jack O'Connor, Pete Brown, and Warren Page. Quiet moments spent daydreaming turned the rabbits I shot into charging grizzlies. Squirrels became man-eating cougars and leopards ready to charge out of the treetops. Like many youngsters of the era, I sent off for every imaginable gun catalog and drooled for hours over the latest rifles and new calibers. I memorized ballistic charts of most of the then common cartridges, like other kids my age studied batting averages of their favorite baseball players and teams.

With the 1960s came increases in our local deer populations, including on our own property. When the deer season opened each fall, however, it was as if a signal was sent directly to the resident deer—alerting them to disappear onto our neighbors' land. I began to despair of ever taking my first white-tailed buck.

By the early 1960s, I was finally considered old enough to hunt on my own. By then, too, .22 rimfire rifles had been outlawed for use on deer, so it appeared I would have to find another "perfect deer rifle." What I "found" was my maternal grandfather's old single barrel 12-gauge shotgun. Perhaps "finding" is the wrong word. I never even thought about taking my first white-tailed buck with any other gun. My grandfather had affectionately named the old

REFLECTIONS ON A FIRST DEER

gun, "the Roar." Many were the times he carried the old gun on squirrel hunts we made together. On rare occasions, as a four or five year old, I had been privileged to carry his gun. Memories of "the Roar" and my grandfather are inextricably linked.

PEAR FLAT PHILOSOPHIES

For the longest time I am sure that my grandfather was convinced that the gun was bewitched. He could hardly ever touch it without a red-haired, freckled-face kid appearing miraculously by his side, ready and anxious to share in a new experience. After my grandfather passed away, the old shotgun became the property of my uncle, who shared the same feeling for the old gun as I did. Somehow I had always felt "the Roar" would play a great role in my deer-hunting career. Thus it was with great pride I accepted the loan of "the Roar" from my uncle.

It seemed like an eternity, but the 1961 hunting season finally arrived. The night before opening day, my dad had rummaged through our supply of shotgun "bullets" and presented me with three 00 buckshot shells. With a certain amount of pomp and ceremony, he issued them to me with instructions to use them wisely. That night I slept little. What little sleep I got, I spent dreaming of whitetails. When the alarm went off, I found that I still had the shotgun shells clutched tightly in my hand. I was out of bed like a shot.

After a hurried predawn breakfast, I dressed in a pair of hand-me-down World War II woolens. Years later whenever I think of those clothes it still makes my body itch all over. But at the time I wore the woolens proudly, like a badge of courage. Well before daylight Dad dropped me at my deer stand, an ancient leaning oak that overlooked a little creek bottom. I tied the old shotgun on a string, which hung from the two by two highseat I would be sitting on some thirty feet above. I then scrambled up the tree to the "seat." Once situated, I carefully pulled up the shotgun. Breaking open the action, I ceremoniously pulled out one of the 00 buckshot shells and slipped it into the barrel. Anticipation was palpable.

Shortly after daylight I heard a shot coming from the direction where I knew my dad was hunting. I closed my eyes and gave a short prayer in hopes that he had connected. Those thoughts had scarcely drifted through my young mind when I heard a scrambling noise. I jerked my entire body in the direction of the commotion, and there I saw it. . . . It was a buck, and he was coming my way! For a moment I forgot I even had a gun. After all those years of dreaming of this moment, finally here was a buck.

REFLECTIONS ON A FIRST DEER

Shaking, I reached up with both thumbs and cocked the hammer on "the Roar." The deer came closer, heading right in my direction. I could see that he might even pass under my stand. I brought the old gun to my shoulder and started pointing it in the direction of the deer. The hardest thing to remember was to put the front bead in the back notch of the receiver. The deer was getting closer, and I was getting nervous. When it looked like the bead and notch were on the little buck's shoulder, I jerked the trigger. The "Roar" belched forth the 00 buckshot. To my delight, the buck went down.

I looked down at my prize and froze. The deer was stirring slightly. Now what? Reload—and fast! I rammed my hands in my pockets, trying to find the other two shells. Then in a moment of panic found them in my right pants pocket. Hurriedly I stuck the shell in my mouth to free both hands and broke open the shotgun. I was so agitated that I pulled the forearm off of the gun, which in turn released the barrel, which then fell thirty feet to the ground below!

This was truly a fine pickle. Here I was, sitting thirty feet above the ground with a 12-gauge 00 buckshot stuck in my mouth, the shotgun's forearm tightly clenched in my left hand, the remainder of the back stock held tightly in my right hand, and my dreams of being a mighty big-game hunter in shreds. The only piece of the shotgun not in my possession lay thirty feet below, albeit not less than three or four feet from the downed buck.

Upon realizing what I had done, now in retrospect, I am surprised I did not bite the shotgun shell in half. After the trauma of the previous few minutes, the crawl down from my perch was accomplished without further drama. With rubbery legs and knees, I simply melted my way down the tree. By the time I gathered up all the important pieces of the ancient shotgun, the young buck had expired. Somewhere up above my granddad must have had tears in his eyes caused by laughter from the antics of his red-haired, freckled-faced grandson. Well, maybe all but one tear was caused by laughter. . . .

Such was my introduction into the world of taking white-tailed bucks. Although I still get excited about taking a deer, I have never again, thankfully, had quite the same experience. When my daughters reached the age where they became interested in guns and rifles, I started them on the road to deer hunting. And I thank the good Lord I was present when they took their first deer. My older daughter Theresa took her first buck when she was eight years of age, while my younger daughter took her first buck when she was but a little older.

Theresa took her buck during one of the worst dust storms we had had in years. By three in the afternoon it was nearly completely dark. Still hunting into the wind, we found an old buck bedded in a cedar thicket. Thanks to the wind and dust, we were able to stalk to within twenty yards. From there she coolly raised the rifle, placed the crosshairs on the buck's shoulder, and squeezed the trigger. It was not until we approached the deer that she started getting a bit weak-kneed.

Me, well I was pretty excited, and I suspect my knees were shaking a bit more than her's. With a grin, showing several missing teeth, she looked my way as we stood admiring her deer. That smile and that moment in time is indelibly branded in my memory, for it was at that moment I realized that I had passed on my heritage to my child—just as my grandfather and father had done for me. I must have been shaking quite a bit and perhaps my color was tainted a bit by the reddish dust. Perhaps dust is what caused the tears in both our eyes. She looked my way and questioned, "Daddy are you all right?" At that moment I could never remember being more all right in my entire life.

Beth's first deer was taken a few years later. At the time I was working for a private ranch operation, where the owner graciously allowed me to take my daughters hunting each year. One cool afternoon we drove the fifty-some miles from our home to the ranch to hunt. Previously we, Beth and I, had spent some time at the range getting her familiar with rifles, scopes, shooting, and learning where a deer's vitals are in relationship to their bodies. No sooner had we settled in the blind than deer started coming by, mostly does and fawns.

Then I saw a buck approaching. My heart started beating and my breathing must have sounded labored to Beth. She looked at me with one of her mother's "You OK?" looks. I whispered, "Beth there's a buck coming our way, a pretty good one. Ease the rifle into position and shoot him right behind his shoulder." I pointed to the direction from which the little buck

REFLECTIONS ON A FIRST DEER

was coming. Like a pro she eased the rifle into shooting position. She pointed the barrel in the direction of the buck and then whispered, "That one, Daddy?" I nodded an affirmative. She peered through the scope, and, when all apparently seemed right to her, she squeezed the trigger of the old 7x57. Immediately the deer went down, and I heard her say, "I got him!"

She looked my way and must not have been too sure of what she saw, for she said: "Dad, are you OK? You're not having a heart attack are you?" I was breathing rapidly and my color was not good—a bit ashen, I was; nevertheless, I reassured her I was going to be just fine in a few moments, and, when I was, we would go see the buck she had just taken. It did not take long for me to recover, and, once I had recovered, I started congratulating her. With something akin to reverence, she said, "I got him, Dad," and just as her elder sister had done, Beth turned to me and smiled, and that precious moment we shared forged a link in the chain between the present and all those loved ones who had gone before us.

Beth's legs were nearly as shaky as mine as we approached the buck. As I watched her caress the antlers and gently stroke the buck's neck, I was reminded of a time nearly twenty-five years earlier when someone else gently touched a small buck's antlers and whispered a small prayer of thanks. There were a few tears shed by the side of each of those three first deer. Both my girls could hardly wait to get back to call their grand-fathers and tell them of their first deer. I knew somewhere above there was another grandfather who, with a tear in his eye, must have shared those first bucks with each of us.

Never Take a Woman Hunting!

Is this the year you have decided to take your girlfriend or wife deer hunting with you? Before you make that daring plunge, there are several things for you to consider . . . namely your ego. During the past many years I have had the opportunity and pleasure to hunt with a great many of the opposite and gentler gender, including my mother and daughters. Luckily I have escaped taking my wife hunting. She enjoys the outdoors, loves to eat venison, but prefers to see me be the one to go afield. To be frank and honest, I'm glad my wife feels that way.

Men, let me put this to you simply . . . the females of our species are generally much better hunters than the males. It is a fact I have long researched. It's also a fact that most men don't like to be upstaged in the hunting arena by their women. Nevertheless, I have found that if you find a female who likes to hunt, you'll find that she's a better shot than most men; indeed, women in general tend to be better shots than we men. Secondly, they do not get as excited as we do over a buck with big antlers (at least not until the animal is on the ground). And thirdly, they approach hunting with an open mind and are not "experts" like we men.

My first involvement with women deer hunters came when I was growing up in the gravel hills just north of the Gulf Coast prairie. In our little rural community of Zimmerscheidt about twenty-five percent of the women hunted deer every year, including my mother. Unfortunately deer were starting to become fairly scarce during the late 1960s and early 1970s because of habitat destruction. My mother loved deer hunting but taking her first buck, well it was quite an ordeal, at least for one of us. Mom had hunted for about six or eight years without ever taking a buck. As the season approached, I was bound, determined, and resolved to see this was going to be her year!

At the time I was working as a wildlife disease specialist. As a regular daily duty I was responsible for catching, subduing, and holding penned white-tailed deer while the project's vets drew blood samples. The strength and agility of these deer are amazing, and, as I learned ways to physically subdue them, they learned ways to counteract my moves. But, as a result, I grew tougher, more agile, and smarter about deer behavior—including how to catch a deer. No big deal . . . it was either learn how to "work" deer or look like I had been in a fight with a buzz saw every day.

As the predetermined "this year Mom takes her first buck" deer season progressed, Mom was again not doing too well. About midway into the season she had still not seen a legal buck. It was not for a lack of trying, either: Mom hunted mornings and evenings, and just about every day of the season. The first weekend of December arrived with a cold Arctic blast, and I headed home to spend the weekend hunting with Mom, Dad, and Glenn, my brother. We arrived at our hunting camp, a half mile behind the house, with about an hour of daylight and hunting time left. Hurriedly we dressed warmly and headed to our respective deer stands, back then simply a few boards nailed high up in huge oak trees to gain a better view of the deer trails.

The wind blew fiercely as I crawled into my normal stand about twenty feet above the ground. I had scarcely gotten settled when I noticed a forkhorn coming my way. In that moment a plan of pure madness developed: I would catch the buck, carry him over to where Mom's deer stand was, and tie him to a tree. Better yet, I said to myself . . . I would tie him by this antlers to the rope hanging from high in the tree—the same rope that she used to pull her gun up with when she had safely crawled into the tree. I squirreled partially down the tree, all the time hoping the wind would cover my sounds and movement and all the while keeping an eye on the deer.

The elements seemed to be working in my favor as I positioned myself on a limb about six feet above the trail that I was hoping the buck would take. On he came, stopping occasionally to pick up a recently fallen acorn. As I quieted my breathing so as not to make a sound, I could feel my heart thumping in my chest and the adrenaline pumping through my body. The buck came nearer, and my labored effort to keep my breathing still became painful. Just as the buck passed directly beneath my position, I got ready to make my move. When he was four steps past directly below me, I jumped. The force of my jump knocked the unsuspecting buck off his feet, but I knew that I had mere moments to make him secure. Quickly I grabbed him, and, thanks to many hours of practice, I secured my hold by wrapping my right arm around his flank, just in front of his hind legs. We wrestled momentarily, but all my practice in the field gave me the edge. I stood up and picked the buck's hind legs off of the ground. He thrashed around quite a bit with his head, but I managed to subdue him completely with my left hand.

Step one was completed! Now all I had to worry about was carrying the nearly 120-pound deer three-quarters of a mile to Mom's deer stand. It took quite a bit of effort, energy, and dogged determination to carry the buck the distance through several briar thickets, across two icy creeks, and through one barbed-wire fence. A weary pair arrived just after dark at the big oak from which Mom hunted. With not so nimble fingers, I tied the buck by the horns to the rope that hung from above, giving the deer just enough room to maneuver around yet not get tangled up in any brush.

With that accomplished, I lay down for about ten minutes—trying to regain enough strength to walk back to my stand, gather up my gear, and get back to camp before Mom, Dad, and Glenn got worried about me. All the way back to camp I giggled to myself, partly over what I had accomplished and partly out of pure exhaustion.

Upon arriving in camp I was asked the usual, "Where you been? What'd you see? What took you so long to get back to camp?" and similar questions. I was hard pressed to keep from smirking, but I managed to make up several stories over dinner about having seen a buck but deciding to pass him up because he was not really notable. I explained away the scratches on my hands and face by telling my folks how I had forgotten a flashlight, which was the inadvertent cause of me having to do battle with a briar thicket on the way home. All in all I thought I played things pretty cool. Just before we turned in that night, I told Mom I thought tomorrow would really be a red-letter day in her hunting career. Am I bad!

Sleep came easily that night. Next morning as we headed toward our stands, we wished each other good luck and departed. About thirty minutes later, just when it was light enough to see, I heard a shot coming from Mom's direction. Sometime later I headed back to camp. I got there just as Glenn and Dad were bringing in Mom's buck. At the same time, several friends of my parents drove up. Excitedly, Dad hollered, "Come look at Mom's first buck."

"That's a nice buck for your first one! Congratulations! How'd you get him?" asked Willy, one of our neighbors.

"You won't believe it!" replied Mom. "I was walking to my deer stand and found him tied to a tree!"

This, of course, was followed by a loud round of laughter. Mom was right . . . nobody believed her. This was my first experience in the ways and manner of women deer hunters, and it taught me a very good lesson: Women deer hunters always tell the truth! Later experience has only confirmed me in this belief. Unfortunately for some men, this little axiom of mine is a decided disadvantage. . . .

I once heard of a fellow who was decidedly not very excited about taking his wife deer hunting. Perhaps it was some internal atavistic caution on his part . . . whatever it was, I never found out, but, I do know the fellow finally decided to take her along and to play a trick on her . . . a trick that was to come back to haunt him.

The story took place during the time I was working the deer check station just north of the South Texas town of Laredo. It had been a rather slow morning, until a very attractive young lady showed up with a huge buck tied across the top of her compact car. The buck dwarfed the car and was one of the best bucks I have ever seen to come out of the South Texas brush country. He had ten very long points, long main beams, better than baseball-bat mass at the bases, which he carried throughout the beams and tines, and he was a solid twenty-five inches wide. It did not take long for a crowd to gather

NEVER TAKE A WOMAN HUNTING!

to admire the beauty of the deer and the attractive young wife. While I recorded the necessary biological data, I asked her about her hunt. Reluctantly she started. . . .

"He's pretty isn't he?" she asked. "I sure hope he was worth it because I guess that buck is going to cause a divorce. . . ." With a lead like that, I was curious to find out more, so I pushed her to fill in all the juicy details.

"Ever since we got married three years ago, I have been after Gil to take me hunting with him. His normal excuse was always something about a deer camp not being the right place for a woman, or I would probably not like hunting anyway and would cause a problem with his friends. Now I don't believe in nagging, but I wanted to see what was so great about going hunting, and I wanted to learn from my husband. So I kept after him. Finally he condescended to take me hunting.

We arrived Friday afternoon just at dark. As we were driving in, we saw what Gil said was a big buck. At least he seemed pretty excited about it. That night I really enjoyed sitting around the campfire and hearing about the bucks and mountain lion one of Gil's friends had seen recently. About 2:30 the next morning, Gil woke me up and said it was time to go hunting. Hurriedly I dressed, put on a minimum of makeup, drank a cup of horrible tasting coffee, and then got in the truck. I asked Gil why we needed to be out so early, and he simply said we needed to get an early start so we would not disturb the deer's morning routine. That sounded fine; after all, what did I know?

Gil insisted I open the gates as we drove to a huge open field without any brush. I could not see any brush, but there was a lot of tall grass. After driving about a mile, we drove up to one tree that Gil called a mesquite. He told me to crawl up the tree, but to be careful because it had a lot of thorns. After I got about halfway up the tree, he told me he'd be back at dark to pick me up. With that he left. But as he was leaving, I thought I heard him snicker and mumble something about hoping this will teach her a lesson, hunting in the No Deer Pasture. . . .

I watched as he drove away and could see the headlights go all the way back to camp. When he reached camp, it was still dark inside the cabin. He shut off the lights, and it was

[19]

nearly an hour later that lights finally came on inside camp. It was another hour before the pickups started leaving. I was beginning to have doubts about my husband and was wondering seriously if I had been set up on a snipe hunt, something I had done when I was in college. . . . Finally, it got light enough to see and I realized I was sitting in the only tree within nearly a mile in any direction. Now I don't know much about deer hunting, but I had always heard Gil talk about hunting in or near thick brush. I must admit watching the sky turn shades of pink was beautiful.

Then about fifty yards away, I noticed some movement in the tall grass. At first I thought it was a dead bush with limbs sticking up. But then I noticed the bush move and stand up. Underneath what appeared to be the bush was a deer. For a second I thought: 'Now there's a smart deer, he's carrying a bush on his head to use as camouflage. . . .' Then I realized it was a big buck. Hurriedly I brought the rifle to my shoulder, got the buck in the scope, and put the crosshairs on his shoulder. That's where Gil had told me to shoot one. And then squeezed the trigger. At the shot the buck went down; he never even kicked.

I carefully crawled from my perch in the tree and walked over to where the buck lay. Once on the ground he was easy to see because his horns were easily visible above the tall grass. I tried to roll him over, but couldn't. I then noticed that I had gotten a little blood on the leg of my trousers. Since Gil had said he would not be back until dark, I decided to walk back to camp, which I could see in the distance. I was there when the men started coming back. They laughed at me about being back so early, taunting me about not being tough enough to hunt. I told them about my buck, but no one believed me. They kept saying something about no one had ever even seen a deer in the pasture I had hunted. I was getting a little mad. Then someone noticed the blood on my trouser leg. Finally they started listening to me.

We drove back into the pasture I had hunted. As we got close to the tree, they could see the buck, and the men started cussing. Some got downright mad that I had taken such a big buck. When we got back to camp it got even worse. I felt even more ostracized than I had before. The level of grumbling in-

NEVER TAKE A WOMAN HUNTING!

tensified. The black looks and snarls continued. Finally I was instructed to pack up my stuff, take my buck, and leave. My feelings were hurt, still are. But I showed them . . . didn't I?"

As to what happened to Gil. . . . I saw the attractive lady who had taken the big buck a couple of years later at an outdoor show where I was doing a deer-hunting seminar. She, on the arm of a man, came up to visit after the program. After

PEAR FLAT PHILOSOPHIES

some casual conversation, she introduced the rather distinguished-looking gentleman at her side as her new husband, Howard, and said: "Howard not only loves to hunt, but he enjoys taking me with him. We just got back from our second African safari. Would you like to see our pictures?" I never did find out what happened to Gil, but it was obvious that she had found a better hunting partner. . . .

Now gentlemen, there are a few morals in all this. Never underestimate a mature white-tailed buck and where you might find him. Never underestimate the abilities of a woman deer hunter, and never, ever put your wife in a No-Deer-Possible Stand!

Horn Rattling I

"Horn rattling" is sometimes described as banging two antlers together and making considerable racket, so as to attract white-tailed bucks itching for a fight—yet, at the same time, carrying out this delicate operation without jabbing oneself with a sharp antler tine. For years it was thought and taught that "horn rattling" worked only in the arid Southwest. To be perfectly frank, it was sometimes dismissed by hunters of other climes as simply another Texas myth. Or, so I thought! On a trip to the Northeast, I learned "horn rattling" was indeed a time-honored technique developed by the aboriginals of old . . . and stolen from them by the teller's distant grandfather or distant-cousin-twice-removed.

Believe what you will, the technique indeed does work at attracting white-tailed bucks in the fall. Why it works really is somewhat of a mystery to me. But I suspect it is similar to a bunch of teenage boys whose hormones have just realized there is more to a young lady than mere obvious outer differences. In trying to impress a pretty young thing, sometimes a shoving match ensues. Suddenly someone yells "fight," and even those who never even intended to get involved in the scuffle dive into the fracas with fists flying. Or possibly even the shoving match got started because someone made an off-color comment about another someone's mother, sister, pet, favorite hunting clothes . . . whatever. During the rut, white-tailed bucks move about, mad at the world and looking for a fight. Well, at least some of the time. . . .

Many years ago my first encounter with horn rattling occurred in my more tender growing-up stage. It occurred just after I had finished reading a story in one of the Big Three outdoor magazines about how fellow Texan, Mr. Bob Ramsey, and a writer rattled up more than twenty white-tailed bucks in a single day. I knew then and there I was going to be a master horn rattler! Unfortunately and in retrospect, I doubt seriously there were a total of twenty bucks, at the time, in our part of Texas. But after reading about what had happened, I became convinced I, too, could rattle up an equal number of bucks if only I had a set of rattling horns. But something told me it was going to take more than the set of five-inch spike horns I had to make sufficient racket to attract an old mossy-horned buck. Just because I was freckle-faced and barefooted did not necessarily mean I was totally ignorant!

After many days of literally combing the woods and bugging my dad and uncles, I was finally able to procure my first "real" set of rattling horns, which came from the skull of a monstrous forkhorn that had ten-inch long beams. As per the instructions in the now tattered magazine, I sawed the antlers from the skull and tied them to a piece of rawhide. Each night before the hunting season, I reread the rattling article until I could right near quote scripture and verse from memory.

Hunting season finally arrived. The first afternoon I crawled into my old oak tree overlooking the narrow creek bottom where I had taken my first white-tailed buck. No sooner had I settled down on the inch-wide seat than I started rattling. I kept it up most of the afternoon, but alas . . . I attracted only a pair of fussy squirrels and one scolding blue jay. When darkness came, I was still convinced the rattling would attract several bucks to the area. That night in camp I told both Mom and Dad of my rattling experience. I told them I was convinced that when I returned to my deer stand the next morning there would be a buck under every bush. After several Jack O'Connor and Warren Page stories, I drifted off to sleep.

Next morning I was up by four to be sure I would be dressed and in my tree at least a couple of hours before first light. I must admit I was somewhat reluctant about walking to my hunting area alone as I was sure that there had to be some rut-crazed buck ready to attack because he had spent all night looking for a fight that had never materialized. Yes, I was convinced of my ability to rattle those horns.

Finally it got light enough to see. Nothing. There was absolutely nothing to see! But hope springs eternal in youth,

HORN RATTLING I

and finally that hope was justly rewarded when two bucks strode into view, one a small forkhorn and the other a small eight-point. Aha! I felt justified . . . even if it had been some fourteen hours since I had last rattled. This, dear reader, is utter conviction!

Now the tattered article took on the same authority as the Bible . . . well nearly, anyway. The article had said that sometimes the really big bucks are slow about coming in; consequently, my reactions to the first cool spells in September would have been totally predictable to anyone who had read the literature. Unfortunately, my truant officer hadn't read the all-important script—I must have driven the poor guy nuts. For as soon as the first late summer days dropped below seventy-five degrees, I headed to the woods, school or no school.

I well remember one cool, drizzly September day. Walking through the woods with my rattling horns strung across my shoulder, I rounded the bend and saw six bucks in a single group peacefully eating on the tender shoots of a yaupon. I seized the opportunity to carve six more notches on my rattling horns, convinced the bucks would come charging in my direction as soon as I started rattling. And charge they did, but not in the direction I had hoped. In less than five seconds they had all bounded away, tails spread wide and held high as they ran. Education is often a disappointing affair.

In time my experience with rattling increased, as did the size of my horns and hunting area. As a budding wildlife biologist working with the Wildlife Disease Project in Texas and taking care of a herd of captive whitetails, I also learned about deer vocalizations. All this was long before anyone even thought of possibly producing a commercial grunt call, so popular these days. As my experience as a wildlife biologist and hunter grew, my territory also expanded to cover most of the Southwest. Perhaps this is how I came to know a gentleman from Houston.

My new-found friend had taken all the game species in North America, most of them true trophies in terms of size and maturity. The only thing he lacked was a large-racked white-tailed deer. Asked to find a ranch where he could take such a buck, I obliged by procuring hunting rights for him on

[25]

a ranch where I had seen two bucks of sufficient antler pro-
portions to grace the listings of the "Book."

We arrived at the Brush Country lease the day after a
"blue norther" had blown with all its fury and the winds were
starting to subside. Conditions "felt right" for hunting one of
the big bucks. The night of our arrival, we made a plan.
Initially my friend wanted me to rattle up the buck for him,
but I finally convinced him that the deer and the experience
would mean a lot more to him if he did the rattling himself.
I also taught him how to grunt like a buck using his own voice,
and I stressed that when bucks really get to fighting sometimes
that they grunt long and hard, not unlike a calf at the end of
a rope being dragged to the branding fire. With that I handed
him my set of "magnum" rattling horns (actually a set of large
shed mule deer antlers with double forks, which closely imitate
two bucks fighting).

HORN RATTLING I

Next morning we headed toward the dry creek bottom where one of the bucks lived. As my friend made his way toward a finger of mesquite that jutted into a prickly pear flat, I gave him some last minute instructions, then I crawled up on the rack on top of our jeep so I could see what would happen. The hunter eased ever so slowly into the mesquite, settled down, and then started rubbing a nearby limb with the antlers. He next, quite naturally, went to grinding the antlers together. From this he went into some serious rattling—I KNEW what was happening, and it still sounded like two bucks trying to kill one another. Then just as I had instructed him to do, he let forth with a deep guttural "Aaaaaaccckk!" So far, so good, I thought complacently to myself.

Just as I was congratulating myself on my excellent teaching skills, I heard the grunt cut short and I saw my friend jump up, throw my horns into the brush behind him, and take off

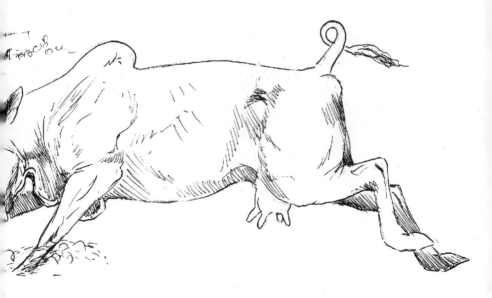

in my direction. I had no idea what was going on. For a moment I thought it possible that he was being attacked by a crazed buck in rut or that he had suddenly seen or nearly sat on a rattlesnake. But here he was . . . running for dear life and yelling "Weishuhnnnnnnnn, you no-count sonofabi . . . !!" Then from out of the brush and right on his tail came the longhornedest, meanest, baddest Brahma cow you ever would want to lay your eyes on.

"Unbeknownst" my friend had set up to rattle right near where a cow had "hidden" her newborn calf. When my friend started his grunting routine, Mama Brahma heard, or so she thought, her newborn bawling. Well I think you can guess the rest. After that fright, my friend forgot all about the big whitetail he was hoping to find; it also took him several years to again build up the courage to grunt like a fighting buck. Somehow, I don't remember the experts ever mentioning a situation like this. . . .

Horn Rattling II

Horn rattling always brings results . . . the problem is that the results are not always consistent with what you may have in mind. With rattling horns in hand, I have attracted myriad wild animals, humans, birds, and even machines.

It was one of those perfect days for rattling, late December, the bucks were in full rut, and the ranch where I was to hunt was home to quite a few mature bucks. My companion that day was someone the ranch owner was anxious to impress, so he had asked me to take out the gentleman and rattle up a buck for him. Just like that—as if I were a magician and able to pull a giant-sized rack out of my hip pocket on demand.

"Rojo," he demanded, "you better rattle up something for this guy or you're not gonna ever be welcome on this ranch again. Comprende? This man owns a huge construction company up north, and, if I'm gonna keep this ranch, I need one of his subcontracts. Comprende?" Being a bright boy, I got his message . . . loud and clear. This was just what I was looking for--a day afield with no pressure.

The ranch we were hunting was relatively free of roads or *senderos* (a cleared lane through the brush), thus I decided to take my hunter into an area near some virgin dense brush with the hope of rattling up a good buck for him. I felt the chances were pretty good no one would have messed with the bucks in these remote places. The hunter seemed an amiable sort of fellow, with little hunting experience, which meant he would likely be more easily impressed if indeed I could rattle up something for him.

Shortly after daylight, we walked for about twenty minutes from the nearest road to get set up next to a dense thicket that bordered a dry creekbed. After finding a spot that felt right,

PEAR FLAT PHILOSOPHIES

I instructed him to face downwind and wait for a buck to come in once I started rattling. Off in the distance I heard the sound of heavy machinery but thought little of it. As I started rattling, the sounds kept getting closer and closer. I rattled louder to counteract the noise, thinking perhaps that would help.

The noise got louder and louder. Just about then a bulldozer, making a seismograph *sendero* broke through the thicket we were watching. I knew I was done for: I just knew my hunting companion would think me to be a complete idiot, and as for the ranch owner . . . well, I really didn't want to think about what he'd have to say. I knew for certain that I would never again be allowed to set foot on his property. And as for my reputation as a horn rattler . . . well, I really didn't want to think about that either! The phrase "forever tarnished" kept going through my head.

HORN RATTLING II

With a sheepish grin, I slowly turned toward my companion as if to give him some sort of explanation, knowing full well he would be totally and eternally "POed." Not a bit. He grinned and over the roar of the bulldozer motor shouted, "Been hearing about how you only rattle up the big ones. Anyone who can rattle up one of those babies out here in the middle of nowhere has got to have talent! Care to show me your exact technique? I'd like to use it next time I need a

'dozer at a construction site! This'll make a better story than shooting a world-record deer!" All I can say is that some people recognize quality when they see it!

Ah, the sweet smell of success! My rattling success has not always been so sweet, nor has the odor. In the past I have rattled up dogs, cats, doe deer, coyotes, bobcats, mountain lions, domestic cattle, myriad crows, ravens, and a fair assortment of "dickie birds." Not to mention having rattled up other hunters, a game warden or two, poachers, and even skunks.

The term "getting skunked" took on a whole new meaning for me while I was hunting on the spacious Nail Ranch. J. Wayne Fears, our guide, Craig Winters, and I were hunting together in hopes of rattling up a good whitetail. When it came my turn to rattle the horns, I selected a long brushy, rocky ridge and instructed Wayne to position himself about twenty yards downwind of me to intercept any bucks that might try circling our position. Craig stayed close to help me make additional fighting whitetail sounds.

No sooner had I started my sequence than Craig and I noticed movement out in front of Mistah Fears. Whatever it was, it was wasting no time in responding to my rattling. Perhaps finally (after several years of trying) I was going to rattle up a big whitetail for my hunting partner. I still could not see what it was, but whatever it was had just parted the tall grass and was heading directly for us. Just about then I saw Fears jump up like he had sat on a scorpion, start backing up, and finally go into full retreat . . . all the time hollering "Git outa here!"

Wayne's back-stepping dance was quickly consuming the twenty yards that had previously separated us. It was only as he got closer that I noticed a low-slung animal running toward us, flashing black and white against the dun-colored background. Just as the visual pattern was imprinting on my mind did the odor hit me. Skunk! And what a smell! The fumes spread over the three of us, enveloping us like a thick woolen blanket. Gagging ourselves sick, we hightailed it out of there . . . all convinced that there'd be no need for additional "skunk scent" for a while! Sometimes my horn rattling smell of success has not been too sweet!

HORN RATTLING II

In the past I have rattled up bucks for a great variety of people including friends, strangers, politicians (where were the skunks when I needed them?), governors, celebrities, cameramen, and even unbelievers—though in the case of the unbelievers, there are some who think the jury is still out when it comes to my rattling abilities. Finally, however, my reputation spread. Of course sending out a publicity flyer to all those who bought hunting licenses in the Southwest and Southeast helped a bit. In time the rumor of my rattling abilities made its way to J. Wayne and Sherry K. Fears (all this long before getting skunked), who booked a whitetail hunt on one of the operations I was managing at the time. My time to shine had finally come!

Wayne had seen bucks rattled up before, but Miss Sherry, well, she was going to take a bit more convincing. "Noooo problem!" I said to myself. We left camp just before daybreak. Eight rattling attempts later and with nothing more to show than skinned-up knuckles, even I was beginning to have my doubts. The afternoon produced only more skinned knuckles and a drooping ego. Never had I had such a bad run of rattling luck. I could see Wayne's confidence in me sagging, but the look in Sherry's eye was unmistakable: "Who is this idiot and what does he know about deer anyway!" Not a very fortuitous beginning.

That night around the dinner table I conveniently changed the subject many times, especially when someone mentioned rattling. After bedtime that night, I spent considerable time praying for some rattling success and evoking the ghosts of O'Connor and Ramsey to help me along my path. Next morning we again started rattling shortly after daybreak, but again, the results were the same: no deer. I was seriously beginning to hate white-tailed deer! Now my honor was at stake, if not the honor of all of Texas.

Thinking these thoughts, I took my pair of unbelievers to the honeyest of my honey holes, the place I had been saving only for emergencies. Boy, was this ever an emergency! I instructed Wayne and Sherry to follow me into the dense thicket to a small opening right in the middle of the thickest part of the thicket. With hand signals, I instructed Sherry to position herself on my right and slightly in front of me, and I motioned

PEAR FLAT PHILOSOPHIES

Wayne to move to my left. Bringing my right index finger to my lips, I motioned for quiet.

I waited about ten minutes until the crickets started chirping and the birds had started singing to begin my rattling sequence. No sooner had I started imitating the pushing and shoving match of two big mature bucks than I heard a ruckus in the thicket, coming our way. Finally I was going to be vindicated. Success would be sweet. The Fears family would return home to write only glowing articles about the greatest horn rattler in Texas, nay, in all the world! I winked a wink of confidence in Sherry's direction.

The noise was coming closer. I could feel the tension growing. In mere moments a huge trophy, a *muy grande* whitetail would step from the brush. Victory and fame were just a few steps behind the edge of the thicket's dense brush. Closer the sound came. With each beat of my heart, my tonsils banged together. Out of the corner of my left eye, I could see Wayne tensing, to the right I saw Sherry slowly raise her rifle in the direction of the sound. "Get ready." I whispered to Sherry. "He's a good'un!"

Suddenly there was an eruption of movement on the thicket's edge coming in our direction. And into the small opening before us charged, in all his flaming glory, a Mexican fighting rooster. Now this rooster, as if to add insult to the injury already inflicted, lit on a mesquite stump right in front of us and started crowing! I had often heard, "It ain't over till the fat lady sings." Well, even my newly found friends had to admit there was something positive about horn rattling. At least I showed them the excitement of rattling horns and that on some rare occasions it certainly is *something to crow about!*

Great Misses

"Son, them that tells you they ain't ever missed a shot at a deer has either done very little hunting or is just plain lying! There ain't nothing wrong or disgraceful about missing. Just try to learn from your mistakes! They'll be plenty of chances in your lifetime at other deer. Gather up your stuff and let's get to camp. Your mom will likely be wondering what's going on. From where she was hunting I'm sure she heard the shot." So spoke my dad after he had listened to my tale of woe as to how I came to miss a shot at a decent buck. "Probably won't be the last one you'll miss," he consoled as we started out of the woods. "I've sure had my share of 'em."

"But Daddy, he was right there not more than. . . ." I protested as I trailed slightly behind my father as we walked toward the camp.

My dad was right on both accounts: That first miss was certainly not my last chance at a buck, nor was it my last miss. As someone who has pursued white-tailed deer from just below the tundra in Canada to well into the Republic of Mexico, I am sad to say there have been several more misses, serious misses if you will. Some hunters spend a lifetime in search of a white-tailed buck that will make the record book and yet never even see one. Me, I have had two chances at a record-book deer. The first one I missed in Mexico and the second in Canada.

A few seasons ago I received an invitation from an outfitter in the Mexican state of Tamaulipas to hunt white-tailed deer. Earlier I had helped him set up some programs in the management of trophy white-tailed deer, and this was his way of saying thank you. "No need to bring anything. We'll have your license and a camp rifle for you, so you do not have to worry about getting firearm permits and all that red-tape paperwork."

Although I liked the idea of not having to mess with the hassle of getting permits, I was reluctant to use an unfamiliar rifle. Indeed, just before leaving for the hunt, I had been asked to do a hunting seminar. One of the points I had really stressed dealt with knowing your rifle and having it sighted in properly. "Know exactly where it shoots at varying ranges. Never allow someone else to sight in your rifle, and never take anyone's word about where he says the rifle is shooting. Always take the time to shoot it yourself, so you can be sure!"

I arrived in camp with about two hours of daylight left. On the way to the rancho, my guide filled me in on a buck one of the vaqueros had seen occasionally. This buck had been observed each time at ten o'clock in the morning crossing a *sendero* (in this case a fenceline right of way) as he traveled from one pasture to another. According to the ranch cowboy, the buck was a *muy grande, si, muy ancho, grande cuernos.* The outfitter had seen him as well and estimated him to exceed the Boone & Crockett minimum.

As I readied for a rushed evening hunt, the ranch guide handed me a .264 Winchester Magnum, topped with variable scope and a handful of cartridges. I mentioned wanting to shoot it to see where it was sighted in. *"No senor. Chuting scares the onnimahls. De reeflay, chutes muy bueno,"* stated the guide making a small circle by touching his index finger to his thumb. *"Ju no chute, but the venaho. No mas cartuches! Ondolay!* We go, *rapido!"*

Even though I knew better, I crawled into the old "Chevvee" and away we went. A mile into the pasture he stopped the truck and speaking as much with his hands said, "Senor Colorado (pronounced cahl-ah-rou). *Este muy grande, donde,"* my guide said as he pointed down the *sendero. "Este . . ."* he began as he reached for a stick to draw a picture in the wet sand. *"Este . . . thrripod! Si? Ju* stay, I go. *Buenos suerte!"* There is no excuse . . . I knew better.

To make a long painful story somewhat shorter, I spent five full days after that first evening sitting in the tripod from before daylight until dark hunting for the potential record-book deer. During those five full days of hunting I saw a grand total of two deer, a doe and her fawn, plus possibly 300 javelina, nearly as many coyotes, and about twenty-five bobcats. Did I happen to mention that during the entire hunt it rained every day, nearly all day long, and that the temperatures hovered just above freezing? Each night the outfitter assured me the buck would in all likelihood cross the *sendero*, probably at ten o'clock the next morning.

On the sixth morning at exactly ten o'clock, I noticed movement in the brush near the fence. My patience was to be rewarded! The rifle came to bear on the deer moving toward the fence. His antlers were huge, everything and more than what the guide and vaquero had said they would be. The scope's crosshairs centered on the buck's shoulder nearly 100 yards distant. From a solid rest I squeezed a shot. In the recoil I lost sight of the buck. When I recovered, he was gone. The shot had looked perfect through the scope. Surely the buck lay only a short distance in the brush. Hurriedly I made my way to where he had stood. There in the wet sand were his tracks, which I followed for nearly a mile. No deer, no blood, nothing. How could I have possibly missed? I was sick. That missed shot ground at me . . . especially after the long wait, solid rest, and soft squeeze.

Dejectedly I walked back to camp. Then, and only then, I took the time to set up a target at fifty yards. The first shot printed nearly eleven inches above the bullseye. The second shot went almost exactly in the same hole. My words to the attendees of the seminar came back to me. "Never trust anyone's word when trying to determine where a rifle shoots. Always know where it shoots before going hunting!" Laughing sickly, I muttered to myself, "Well the guide was right about two things: The buck did cross the fence at ten o'clock in the morning and he did say the rifle shot a tight group. He just didn't say where!"

My second chance at a record-book deer occurred not very far from Carrot River, Saskatchewan. After several days of hard hunting in near-zero degree weather, our guides jumped a big buck out of a dense thicket along a creek bottom. I was positioned on a pasture road that bordered the thick bottom. When I first saw the buck, he was about 500 yards away running as hard as he could directly in my direction. I could feel excitement course through my body as I began to get ready. When the distance closed to about 450 yards, the buck started bouncing from one side of the road to the other as if he was looking for a way to get back in the brush.

Hurriedly I tried to get in a sitting position, but immediately I lost sight of the deer. Next I jumped up and tried to get a rest on a nearby tree, but again I could not see the buck. The only way I could see him was to stand in the middle of the road on two very shakey legs. The moment of truth was at hand. It would have to be an offhand shot or nothing. Holding as steady as possible under less-than-ideal conditions, I estimated the distance to be 350 yards, and I squeezed the trigger.

At the shot, the buck disappeared into the brush to my right, which was a brushy fenceline abutting a huge field. Less than two seconds later, I heard a second shot and a solid "whomp." I can tell you exactly how big that buck was and where it ranks in the record book because my compadre of many hunting trips, Gary Machen, cleanly took the buck only moments after I missed him. That is how I came to miss my second chance at a book deer. Will there be a third chance? *Quien sabe?* Certainly I would like to think so! I am sad to say, but there have been other misses as well. . . .

Like the time I hunted on the spacious Nail Ranch in northwestern Texas. My guide for the hunt was a gentleman named Dan Walker. Dan earns his keep as an officer with the Department of Public Safety, which is a fancy way of saying he is with the highway patrol. He also is a firearms instructor for his department, never fails to shoot a perfect round with handgun or rifle, and does shooting exhibitions; in short, he's someone you might call a "top gun." The first day afield I told him about my past misses with big bucks, which included the two sorrowful tales aforementioned.

I could see one of those looks cross his face as if to say: "Oh no, not one of those guys that can't shoot." Five shots later and three missed bucks, we headed back to camp for lunch. That afternoon after ten more missed shots, we headed back to camp for more cartridges. The next morning I proceeded to miss ten more shots. At that point Dan started questioning me: "Have you ever really hunted in the past? Have you actually shot a buck or have you just had your picture

GREAT MISSES

taken with bucks shot by other guys?" Actually, given my performance, I thought Gary was showing admirable restraint—even though his words were a bit acidic.

After another couple of misses, he started in with, "Well shall we go see if you can miss another one?" Which I did. "Why stop now? You still have about ten more cartridges with you." Which I shot at running bucks. "You keep this up and two things are definitely gonna happen: You're either going to run out of cartridges and money, or I'm gonna apply for the lead mining rights on this ranch!" This he followed with an even more bemused, "Care to try for the ranch record for misses?" After a few more missed shots, he said, "I think you have now taken sole possession of the most misses in the history of this ranch, probably the county, and may have even established a new state record!"

Hey, what could I say but to quote an old Jerry Reed song, "When you're hot you're hot, and when you're not you're not!" It all comes down to what my father had told me years earlier, "Them that's claimed they ain't ever missed a deer has either not hunted very much or they are lying!" But he had also suggested I learn from my mistakes. I have! The next time I have Dan Walker as a guide, I will make him do the shooting. And he will miss, even if I have to load his handgun with blanks!

Remembering Tobe

The annual hunting camp meeting of the Grand Slam was called to order. Permanent chairman, Bob Parker, Jr., called the roll. Tom, Steve, Jim, Bob, Buddy, and Larry all acknowledged their presence with an appropriate sign or grunt. Opening the floor to new and previously undiscussed business, Bob, Jr. asked "Wonder where the mystery buck is tonight? Any of you guys got a plan?"

Buddy interjected, "I want Tom to explain how he happened to shoot a turtle on a quail covey rise! Did you know he ate an entire covey of quail for dinner last night?"

Jim continued the new business discussion by demanding "I want to know who was responsible for releasing that black snake in my bedroom!"

Tom countered, "I've got two questions! Who put catsup on mmmyyyy steaks? And who replaced mmmyyy expensive dinner wine with Ripple?" Red, the ranch manager, chuckled.

Steve continued the discussion with, "I think we ought to all start riding mountain bicycles whenever we leave camp. Hey! We could cover them with Bushlan!"

Guest, Jay Gates, looked over my way and asked, "Larry Weishuhn, do you know how to ride a bike?" I must have had a blank stare on my face, for he gave me a funny look.

While my body was seated at the meeting table, my mind drifted back a couple years earlier to the day I had finally taken ol' Tobe. Actually the story started several years before that fateful day, seven to be exact. Tobe (pronounced with a long "o" and silent "e") had not really been the buck's name to begin with. Actually my first gasps upon seeing the deer were several expletives, not necessarily the kind one would use in mixed company or that were very complimentary of a buck with such a rack.

PEAR FLAT PHILOSOPHIES

I first saw old Tobe from the helicopter that we used to conduct our annual game survey. When we passed over a dense thicket, out popped a white-tailed buck. His antlers had massive, wide-spread beams with ten long tines going up, and two drop-tines going down. He was the kind of buck one normally only sees in ones dreams. The heavy-necked buck bounded about ten yards before again disappearing into the dense thicket. Even though I hunted hard for the buck that first season, he was nowhere to be seen. After the season closed, the vaquero on the ranch told me he knew of the buck, but only on very rare occasions had he even caught sight of him. Because of the size of his body and rack, I estimated him to be a mature five year old.

The following October I again saw the buck, in the same area close to a remote water hole. If anything he was even bigger than the previous year, but this year he had a total of three droptines, ten long points going up, with what I guessed to be a twenty-five inch spread. Again, I got to see him only briefly. When the season opened, we hunted him at every opportunity, yet he evaded all human eyes. He didn't get to be that size because he was stupid.

A year later as we took off from the ranch's headquarters in the helicopter, I wondered if we would see Tobe. I thought of him as THE BUCK. During the survey, we tried to find him but failed. I was beginning to wonder if he had fallen prey to a pack of coyotes or possibly the cougars, which frequented the same brushy draws that he seemed to favor. But after the hunting season was over, the vaquero told me of a buck that had to be THE ONE, based on the description of his antlers and where he had seen him. *"Si, esta macho viejo!"* assured the ranch cowboy. It was from that spring that THE BUCK became ol' Tobe.

It was the buck's characteristics that led me to name him ol' Tobe. During the years I was growing up, an elderly black man lived up the creek from us. Tobe looked and was old from the first time that I can remember him coming over to work cattle with us. Thirty-seven years later and still occasionally helping neighbors work cattle, he had changed very little. The white-tailed buck I hunted was similar to his namesake. Even as he advanced in years, he did not change. Neither his antler style nor his sharpness and elusiveness, just like the original, my old friend, Tobe. I could think of no more appropriate or honorable name than ol' Tobe.

The next few years I saw Tobe only one time during our game surveys. His antlers were still as impressive as the first time I had seen him, but the years had started taking their toll on his body. Then we quit seeing him. Even the vaquero suspected the old buck might have succumbed to advanced age, bad

teeth, and hungry predators. The thought of hunting without the hope of taking the old buck left me feeling a bit empty and sad. Through the years Tobe had become a special friend.

"Why don't you and Warner hunt together this afternoon?" said Bob Jr. pointing to Steve Warner and me. "Reckon there'll be a buck safe on the entire ranch with two biologists hunting together?" kidded our pal, Buddy.

Steve and I spent most of the afternoon riding in the back of a high-racked pickup looking for deer but at the same time chatting amiably and discussing the design of a new camo pattern that Steve had in mind. As the afternoon wore on and evening approached, we had about thirty minutes of daylight left. "Where you wanna go?" queried Steve. I thought for a moment, and then for some unknown reason I suggested we try the area near the remote water hole where we had seen ol' Tobe in years past. Just before the day's end of legal shooting time, we walked to the top of the dam and peered off the backside. About seventy-five yards distant, a movement caught our eyes.

Hurriedly Steve brought his binoculars to bear on the spot. I looked for a solid rest in case the buck was worth taking. "He's definitely mature." whispered Steve, then continued, "He's over twenty inches and has at least one kicker on his back tine. . . . I don't know. Wait a second, I think he's got something either hanging down or growing down from his right antlers. By golly it's a drop-t. . . ."

Before he finished saying drop-tine, I squeezed off a shot. Immediately the buck went down. I looked at Steve and asked: "Do you think it could be?"

"I don't know. We haven't seen him for the past two years. But that buck sure looked old and gray. Could be," he replied.

The two of us scrambled down the tank dam, nearly falling on our heads in our haste to get to the deer. Approaching the buck, I noticed not one but three drop-tines growing downward from the buck's right antler. He had ten points going up, one kicker on his back right tine, and an additional four long points around his bases, giving him eighteen total points. The buck's muzzle was gray as was the patch on his forehead. Around his face, neck, and brisket was a lot of loose

REMEMBERING TOBE

skin, generally a sure sign of older age in deer. After inspecting and admiring his antlers, I held open the buck's mouth so Steve could get a better look at his teeth, which I knew were worn to the roots after having run a finger over his smooth gums. "That's the oldest buck I have ever tried to age," commented Steve. "Same here," said the biologist part of me.

"That's got to be your ol' Tobe buck!" enthused Steve as he reached to shake my hand in congratulations. "After all these years, you finally did it! Well done!

Looking at his body and the condition of his teeth, it was obvious that ol' Tobe would not have survived much longer. Probably in a month or two he would have been coyote bait. That night, long after the rest were dreaming of the morrow and the promise of big bucks it would bring, I sat staring into the last glowing embers of mesquite coals and remembering Tobe.

"Hello! Larry Weishuhn, are you there?" shouted Jay Gates in my ear. "Do you know how to ride a bicycle?"

"Yes, it has to be ol' Tobe. . . ."

"Oh, Noooooo, everybody. Larry here is off again—daydreaming about ol' Tobe!" shouted Tom to the others.

"Come back, Larry! We need to discuss new business—we haven't even gotten to the old business part of the meeting yet!"

The Tale of the Wide Buck

Beneath us stood a buck. What an understatement! The buck was wider than any whitetail I had ever seen. He was not at all spooked by the helicopter that hovered only a few feet above his majestic rack of antlers. His regal, impassive stare bored into us, telling us in body language that we were nothing more than a temporary nuisance. Hastily I snapped a few still photos and we continued on our way to complete the rest of the game survey.

At the time of seeing the old buck, I commented to the pilot that the buck looked liked he easily had a thirty-inch spread. His antlers were not only wide but possessed considerable mass, and he had long tines as well, an unusual combination for wide whitetail racks. I felt as if I somehow knew the old buck. For the past several years, I had seen a similarly shaped buck in the same general area. If indeed he was the same buck, this year he was simply outstanding. Each year upon seeing what I suspected was the wide deer, I mentally marked his location and silently hoped he would appear again during the following year's helicopter game survey. Annually he obliged.

I kept his location a secret from the hunters on the property. But when his age became advanced and he put on the extremely wide rack, I decided to share my secret. My hope was that one of the hunters would take him rather than him being pulled down by coyotes. It would be a shame for such a magnificent rack to be gnawed upon by rabbits and rats. The year the buck put on his widest rack and about two or three weeks before the season opened, I gave a program to the hunters on the ranch about the upcoming season. During the presentation, I showed them slides of the wide buck.

PEAR FLAT PHILOSOPHIES

My audience was flabbergasted: Most could not believe their eyes, for they had never seen such a wide rack. I pinpointed the general area where every fall I had seen him during our helicopter surveys, showing them on a map the dense creek bottom in the northern portion of the ranch. I told my enthusiastic audience that I had watched the wide deer grow up and was afraid that, if he was not taken this fall, he would become the meal of the coyotes or perhaps a mountain lion, which inhabited the ranch. I wished each of the hunters the best of luck, instructing them that if they should happen to take him that I wanted to know immediately so photographs could be made to document the "wide one." With that I left, wondering if indeed the old buck would be taken, or perhaps even be seen.

In the past I had seen a few really big deer while doing helicopter game surveys throughout the Brush Country, but alas less than one-tenth of one percent were ever harvested by hunting. About halfway through the season, I stopped by the camp to visit with the hunters. They had seen some pretty fair "*muy*

grandes," but the wide buck continued to elude them. Several had already decided that, if by Christmas the buck had not been seen or taken, they would start doing deer drives to push the old buck from his cover. I wished them luck and left.

Five days after Christmas, I again visited the ranch. As promised, several of the hunters had already begun conducting a series of intense deer drives. The hunters had enlisted the help of families, friends of families, and anyone who could hobble. Essentially their strategy was to walk hand-in-hand across the pasture where the wide deer had previously been spotted. Good bucks were flushed from cover, but never the "wide one." Everyone had his own personal reason and excuse, which ranged from "he's too smart for us" to "probably a poacher has slipped in and taken the buck" to "the biologist photographed the buck on someone else's place and is having a good laugh on us." By the time the season ended, the "wide one" had still not been seen.

After the season I happened to be in the neighborhood of the ranch, which incidentally is surrounded by a high fence— all 15,000 acres of it. When I arrived, no one was at the big house where the hunters spent their nights and mid-days, so I drove an extra 300 yards to the caretaker's house, which is a simple ranch house and home to an elderly Mexican couple who take care of chores for the hunters and work for the ranch owner outside of hunting season. As I approached, Senor Juan waved me into the house. Before I could even sit down, his wife graciously poured me a cup of steaming hot coffee sweetened to saturation with sugar, typical of the Brasada. We exchanged pleasantries about the weather, I asked about their son who lived in San Antonio, and I asked what they had planned for their Christmas visits.

During a lull in the conversation, I remembered a photo I had in my briefcase of the wide buck I had seen the previous fall. Upon showing him the photo, I asked Senor Juan if the hunters had taken him during the season. He smiled and simply said "No, Senor Colorado."

Then I asked the old gentleman if he had ever seen the buck. He smiled broadly and replied, *"Si Senor! He ees me compadre!* He feeds with my *caballos* every evening. He lives between my *casa* and that of the *cazadoros."*

PEAR FLAT PHILOSOPHIES

The caretaker went on to explain how each year, about a week or so before the opening of the hunting season, the wide buck would show up at his house. Every afternoon the buck would eat corn with his horses, literally within a stone's throw of where the hunters lived during the hunting season. It is quite likely that each day the old buck would watch the hunters as they drove past where he lay with the old man's horses—on their way to where the "wide one" was supposed to be living! All the while the hunters, their families, and anyone who could hobble along formed a human cordon to find the wide buck, the wily old soul had lived within a quarter of a mile of everyone!

The caretaker then told us how in mid-February the buck would disappear until the following first week of November, when he again would show up every afternoon to be fed with the horses. Senor Juan was certain the wily old wide one lived quite nearby during the hunting season. I sat enthralled by the elderly gentleman's tale. His wife stood by his side smiling and gently nodding. Finally I could stand it no longer.

"Senor Juan, why did you not tell the hunters about where the buck lived? I am sure they would have paid you handsomely for the information."

"No, no, Senor Colorado, you do not understand. The *viejo macho*, he is *me compadre!*"

But I did understand!

Greenhorn Cameramen and Directors

It was a perfect setup. With any luck at all we would wrap up the filming of the video this afternoon. Less than fifty yards away stood a big mature buck. Unlike the norm for his kind, he stood in an open area, trying to be a star. The sun was shining from over my shoulder, illuminating the entire scene. It was an eerie light, like you would expect just before a serious wet front. The dark almost grayish green clouds foretold what the next several days would bring. Everything was ready, and the timing and lighting couldn't be better.

I glanced back at the cameraman for one final check before crawling the last four or five yards to make the shot. Trying to ignore the camera as much as was earthly possible, I crawled forward, readied the double-barrel .58 caliber Kodiak muzzle loader rifle, and was drawing a final bead when I heard, "SSSSSSSSSSS!" from over my left shoulder. For a moment I was hesitant to turn around, thinking perhaps there might be a rattlesnake about to strike.

"Don't shoot!" stage-whispered the cameraman.

"Don't shoot??? What do you mean, don't shoot? I whispered frantically back—we've been waiting for a setup like this for the past two weeks! This buck is huge and will easily make the Longhunter Society record book! What do you mean don't shoot?"

Behind me there was silence. "We're out of tape," finally came the answer.

"Well, put in another one. If we don't do something in the next few moments, we're gonna loose our chance at this buck, and with that front coming, chances are it's gonna rain for the next four days." We'd already been at this for two weeks, so I knew that it was now or never. "For cripes sakes replace the tape and let's get on with the program!"

"Can't! . . . I left the rest of our tapes back at camp."

While all this was going on, the buck moved even closer. He was perfect: He had massive bases and long tines, with pearling all the way out to the tips of his tines. I wanted that buck. As I started to shoot the buck anyway—video camera or no—I remembered with a flash that we needed to complete the video program we had started. In another flash I remembered that I had one deer tag in my pocket, and it needed to be used on a deer I took for the camera. Under my breath I mumbled all sorts of bad things about cameras, dead batteries, video programs, and my involvement. Stoically I watched as the big buck drifted into the nearest thicket. At least I thought I was being stoic.

The making of a high quality hunting video program is hard, tedious work, and there is much more involved than most hunters realize. It's not simply a question of taking a home video camera and going out and taping your hunting partner. In the past it has been my pleasure to have worked with several professional videographers, such as Jerry Smith and a few others who understand the interplay between the camera and the hunting of wildlife. Camera people such as Jerry are rare. He is a perfectionist, but he knows wildlife and he knows what must be done and how to accomplish a difficult wildlife and hunting assignment. There are a few others who have that same rare talent, but there aren't many. There are legions of cameramen out there who know the camera but who lack an understanding of either hunting or wildlife. Legions.

I recall one cameraman we worked with for a short period of time who was addicted to nicotine. He smoked constantly. We would set up for a hunting scene in an area where deer came everyday to feed on acorns, and, as soon as we moved into the area, the deer would move out. If we finally would get a deer interested in coming our way and just as he would start coming, it was as though it were some sort of signal for this guy to light up another cigarette. Finally we had to ship him out!

Then there was this other cameraman who kept forgetting to cover up or turn off the little red light that shines on the front of the camera whenever it is in operation. Normally this is to alert the "talent" in front of the camera to be on his or her best behavior. Well, this particular film was of a turkey hunt, and that little red light certainly got a lot of attention from the turkeys—all the wrong kind of attention! To be honest, it was one of those years when even Rio Grande turkeys were reluctant to respond to calls, so at first we didn't suspect a human source was complicating our task. Our task seemed Sisyphean: We would finally get gobblers to respond to our calls, they would approach, but then for some undetermined reason they would spook just before getting in range. This had happened with frustrating regularity—five times to be exact—when finally my hunter who was in front of the camera with me happened to turn and look back at the camera. There it was . . . a fancy little red light just-a flashing and shining for all it was worth. A little red light for all the gobblers in turkeydom to vamoose . . . and fast!

Perhaps one of my more interesting incidents of dealing with camera people happened a few years ago. The director on this particular shoot had recently graduated from a university that issued degrees in "telecommunications." His outdoor camera and directing experience up to that date had dealt with shooting a program about tournament archers; moreover, he had grown up in an urban environment where pigeons in the park were considered wildlife. Hunting experience? This man had never hunted anything beyond his first cup of coffee and newspaper in the morning. As a director he was demanding, and he was completely green when it came to wildlife—especially mature white-tailed deer.

I had become involved in the production he was doing because a *friend* had recommended me as someone who might be able to rattle up a buck for the camera. Those of us who hunt for mature, large-racked white-tailed deer realize how difficult it is to bag such a buck. If you agree, read on! So now that we've established the difficulty of procuring a good specimen, let's now throw in a couple of cameras and operators to run them, a sound man with a bunch of gear, a director, a "guide," and a hunter. All this adds up to a total of five humans, but not just any humans—humans who have enough gear to fill the back of a pickup bed.

PEAR FLAT PHILOSOPHIES

With that in mind we set up a rattling and hunting scene. Finally all was ready. Off in the distance the serenading coyotes announced the beginning of another December, Brush Country day. Birds chirped and sang as the sunrise infused the sky with shades of oranges and yellows. And, as if on cue, a slight northerly breeze began blowing. I glanced at the person just

ahead of me. He was fully camouflaged and in the early morning haze appeared more like a bush than a hunter. His arrow was nocked and ready. A backward glance revealed the two cameramen, the sound man, and their gear were equally camouflaged. The director silently looked on from his rearguard position.

"This just might work," thought I, full of confidence. I had just gotten a tight grip on my Magnum rattling horns when I felt a tap on my shoulder. It was the director.

"In this scene," spoke he in a normal speaking voice, "I want you to rattle up a big buck, and I want you to rattle him to right there," and he pointed to a dead mesquite snag about ten yards away. With instructions to the uninitiated completed, he nodded his head, turned, and walked back to his position.

While I was waiting to let all the deer in the county forget we were there, I felt something hit my back like a thrown pebble. Turning around I saw the director make a furious motion with his hands, obviously instructing me to start rattling. I rolled my eyes, but obeyed by starting the rattling sequence with rubbing the bush in front of me, softly grunting, waiting a bit, and then grunting some more. With these preliminaries done, I issued forth a snort-wheeze, a sound similar to "fit-fit-fit-fffeeeeeeee," typical of one buck telling another, "Buster if you don't leave right now I'm going to whip you all over this place."

Shortly after bringing the antlers together and meshing the tines, I saw movement to our left. Not only was it a buck, it was a tremendous twelve typical point with nearly a twenty-four-inch spread. He came our way, proud in his stance and gait yet supremely cautious. He just kept on coming. I knew the cameramen must be getting a full tape of this buck. The lighting looked perfect, and the breeze was so slight that it should not have been picked up by the microphones. At the same time, the sound man should be getting the coyotes howling in the background, the cardinal chirping overhead, and the sounds I was making with the rattling horns. All seemed perfect.

The buck walked to within fifteen yards of our position but not quite to the mesquite snag the director had pointed out before we started. I knew any second the hunter would come to full draw, and we would be able to film the taking of a monster whitetail. Greater caution was replacing the buck's curiosity and desire to come to the fight. He stopped, stared directly at our "entourage," then stamped his right foot. The moment of truth was at hand. The buck turned to go, and I started grunting. With that he stopped and turned broadside, around seventeen yards away.

Still the hunter did not come to a full draw. I shook my head as if to clear it—surely it's not possible to have a nightmare and be fully awake? By this time the buck had seen enough and trotted into the brush. Shaking my head again, I leaned forward to the bowhunter and whispered, "Why didn't you shoot?"

Before he could answer, the director stormed forward, stopped right in front of the dead mesquite snag, pointed to the ground, and with a loud voice said, "Mister Weishuhn, I thought I told you to rattle up a buck and have him stop right here (pointing at the ground). Obviously you are not as good at this rattling business as we were lead to believe. Now!" he said emphatically, "I want you to do as you are told and rattle that buck back up and have him stop right here, on this very spot! Do you understand! We will never complete this project if you do not do as you are told!"

Right. . . . Movie people, don't you just love 'em?

Vittles

"I'm starving. Why I could probably eat a horse, or even that pack mule tied out there!"

In a hunting camp those seem to be pretty familiar statements. Quite honestly, when you're hungry, even an old mule might taste good if properly prepared. Who knows? Ever notice how food seems to taste better in a hunting camp? The phenomenon is one of Nature's greatest mysteries how even the dullest of meals after a hard day afield turns into an epicurean's delight. Maybe most hunting-camp meals taste better because, while away from the cares of jobs, finances, and the world, we tend to forget about the cholesterol content, polyunsaturated fats, and all those other evil things that are bad for us, but make the food taste so good. Or perhaps food tastes better in camp because after a long hard day afield we are just "plain Jane hungry"!

In making such a statement, I know there have been a few camps where the food could have stood a little improvement. I have experienced a few of those myself. Several years ago a couple of friends and I hunted on a ranch just north of the Rio Bravo. The first day in camp one of the other two happened to make a statement about how much he enjoyed eating beans. Care to guess what we had for breakfast, lunch, and dinner every day thereafter? For five straight days we ate beans! I had no earthly idea there were so many dishes in which beans were the only ingredient! Thankfully I stayed in a room by myself, but even that was bad enough!

One year David O'Keeffe, an ace white-tailed deer guide and old hunting partner, and I journeyed to the flat-tops just east of Grand Junction, Colorado. To keep from spooking the mule deer near camp, we decided to maintain a cold, dry camp (meaning no cooking or morning coffee). Since both O'Keeffe and I were partial to fried chicken, we bought enough of the fowl to keep us in meals for five days of hunting. Did I mention the word "fowl"? Perhaps I should have spelled it "foul!" That was certainly the way we felt about fried chicken after four days of eating it three times a day. Ever eat fried chicken twelve times in four days? I don't recommend it.

There are all kinds of hunting camp cooks, some good and some bad. I have watched Roy Bamberg, ace elk tracker and part-time mule jockey perform miracles in cast-iron Dutch ovens as he prepared Mulligan stew, cherry cobblers, and biscuits so light and airy you had to weight them down with gobs of butter just to keep them from floating off your plate. Roy and I often shared cooking duties on our group hunts. This was great . . . for a time. He liked to cook; I liked to cook and eat.

But beware of the cook who grows tired of cooking for a bunch of hunters—especially when that cook feels that his cooking expertise is growing at the expense of his own personal hunting time.

This happened to Roy and me. At first we didn't pay much attention, but after a while we started noticing all the cooking we were doing was seriously cutting into our hunting time. To rid ourselves of cooking duties, we devised a plan. In the presence of the entire camp, Roy and I made a big "tadoo" about gathering mule berries near the hitching post. These we loudly proclaimed would be the key ingredient for that night's supper. All in camp had a good laugh.

That evening the two of us announced we would stay in camp and prepare a feast for the group, as token of our appreciation for having received continual kitchen duty. While the others hunted, Roy and I busied ourselves slicing jalapeño peppers in such a manner that they could easily pass for green beans. Next we started a pot of stew, rich in aroma with a lot of vegetables for color. For a salad we gathered anything in the pasture that looked green, including grass, weeds, tree leaves, whatever. Emily Post would have been proud of the way we set the table, complete with napkins, several forks, and even candles.

VITTLES

When our campmates returned just after dark, they hurried to the table. The aroma of the stew wafted through camp. The cherry cobbler in the Dutch oven had the group salivating like Pavlov's dogs. Once all were seated, we served each some "salad." No one seemed interested. It was the aromatic bubbling stew that held everyone's attention. "Bring on the savory!" they shouted. We nodded, but insisted they first try a helping of our specially prepared green beans. We gave each man a large helping, completed with a chunk of salt pork. (I was surprised that the salt pork didn't burst into flame—so hot had the jalapeños turned the pork!) A few bites of the green beans left the diners scrambling for water and anything else that was cold and wet. Yet no one complained or said a discouraging word. Next came the stew, which Roy whisked to the table with all due pomp and ceremony. Setting the much-awaited main course before the others, Roy made as if to add a final ingredient, what he termed his *pièce de resistance*: the mule berries! Chairs flew backward as hunters raced to get out of the tent. Next morning a couple of the other hunters volunteered to do some of the cooking. Is it not purely amazing what miracles can be performed with a little Aggie ingenuity, some green food dye, and shredded wheat cereal?

In my opinion one of the finest chefs in the Southwest and possibly all of North America, camp or otherwise, is a gentleman by the name of Matt Martinez. Matt's fame as a chef precedes him no matter where he travels. But Matt is also one who enjoys a good joke. For several years he had been doing most of the cooking in his hunting camp. One year he too decided, "Enough was enough." He started laying a plan.

Matt's camp was known far and wide for his great camp cuisine. Neighbors and even strangers frequented his camp as dinner guests during the hunting season. According to Matt, there were times he had nearly as many people eating at his hunting camp as he did in his restaurants. As Thanksgiving approached, Matt let it be known he would be in camp the day after the holiday. The news quickly spread. . . .

On his way to the hunting camp, Matt found a dead buzzard on the road. At that point, his plan blossomed. He chopped off the buzzard's head, wings, and feet and placed them in a bag, discarding the rest. Once inside the ranch, he shot a turkey, dressed it, and put the entrails in the bag with the buzzard parts. He then proceeded to camp.

Fortunately, when he arrived, no one was there. Hurriedly he prepared the feast, using the turkey to make several delicious dishes. The sack with the buzzard parts and turkey entrails were placed next to the stove. Shortly after dark, the hungry hunters arrived, anticipating the feast Matt had prepared for them. The news of Matt's presence in camp had spread through that part of the country, so there were hunters, friends, and strangers seated around the big table.

VITTLES

"Whatta we havin' tonight?" queried several hunters.

"It's an old family secret, handed down to me by my great grandmother. She used to talk about it and how she prepared this dish when times were hard and mouths were plenty. Best as I recall she called it "*zopillote*, or something like that," replied Matt with a wave of his hand.

The guests were served, they began to eat, and the compliments were heaped. Soon most of the men there began asking for the recipe so they could have their wives fix this glorious dish too. Matt said nothing, responding only to their compliments and queries with a sly grin.

Once Matt saw that some of his "guests" were finished eating, he suggested that since he had gone to all the trouble of preparing the meal, the least they could do was take out the garbage. Immediately several volunteered. What these volunteers didn't know, however, was that Matt had earlier moistened the bottom of the paper garbage bag so it would be sure to tear when moved. No sooner had a volunteer lifted and carried the bag a few steps then the bottom ripped open and out fell numerous buzzard parts. The room grew silent, and a mixture of horror and shock was plainly visible on the faces of the diners as they all stared at what they thought they had eaten. Then en mass, they jumped up and started bolting for the doors, windows, and bathrooms—all the while clasping their mouths and stomachs.

As I said, "Beware of the cook who grows tired of feeding his hunting buddies. . . ." There might be a moral in this little tale . . . maybe, maybe not. I just know that in the future I intend to be more careful about making statements such as, "Why I'm so hungry, I could eat a horse!"

The Trouble with Javelinas

The javelina, pronounced *hav-ah-leena,* is an interesting piglike critter that lives in the harsh, arid, cactus-and-thorn country of the Southwest. His kind is sometimes called the musk hog because of the scent gland on his back, located just forward a bit of his stubby tail. The fluid produced by this gland has an unforgettable odor all its own.

By nature the javelina, more properly called the collared peccary, is a gregarious creature. His food habits consist primarily of prickly pear and other cactus, acorns, pecans, and whatever else he can forage. The reputation garnered by the javelina is a bad one. The early western pulp writers portrayed the diminutive javelina equal in ferociousness to a grizzly bear with a bad toothache, but to these authors, the javelina was even worse because these porky little tough guys always travel in herds. In those early writings many an evil villain fell prey to or was torn to shreds by marauding herds of javelina. Not a particularly pleasant picture.

While this image might be an exaggeration, the javelina is no teddy bear either. The elongated upper and lower canine teeth of the javelina sharpen each other with each opening and closing of the mouth. Because of their teeth arrangement, there is no sideward movement of the jaws, only up and down. The result is razor-sharp teeth! Unless cornered, thoroughly perturbed, or teed off at the world, the javelina normally goes about his business "with malice toward none." But get his dander up and watch out! He then becomes a whirling ball of muscle, bristles, and Gillette razors that can move with a quickness that defies lightning. Many a dog, trained for hunting birds, has fallen under the spell of the musky odor and paid dearly for the error.

PEAR FLAT PHILOSOPHIES

Javelina are fighters. When cowdogs are used to herd cattle, they are as much an enemy to the javelina as the coyote or mountain lion, but there has been many an absent-minded ranch dog that has wandered into a small herd of javelina and has paid for the fatal mistake with his life. And woe be to the incautious hunter who unthinkingly strides up to his kill— only to learn of the javelina's tenaciousness the hard way. This little desert devil may look dead, but it's always better to make sure before you get too close.

A few years ago a friend of mine suddenly decided one day that he wanted to go hunting with a handgun and that it was the javelina he wanted to hunt with his soon-to-be purchased sidearm. When this urge hit, he streaked to his favorite store, bought a Thompson/Center Contender in the .22 K Hornet, and thirty minutes later called to announce he was on his way south and would be there in about four hours.

"Go find me some javelina. I've got the urge to shoot a boar. I don't want any excuses. Javelina season is open year around in your part of the country, and you owe it to me to take me hunting! See you at two this afternoon!" Before I could even "gee" or "haw," he had hung up the phone.

The javelina is best hunted by not hunting it at all, so my friend's call left me in something of a quandary. Go hunting a trophy buck, and they are everywhere you go, but go hunting for a javelina, and you might just as well be hunting for woolly mammoths. The results are about the same.

Chuck arrived about an hour before dark. The late January day had been cold and gray, but with less than an hour of daylight left the sun broke out, making the brush, ground, and even the prickly pear cactus look as though they had been touched by King Midas. The late afternoon warmth must have brought the javelina out of hiding. At the first bend of the pasture road, we found a small herd. Chuck hollered "Whoa!" and even before I could come to a complete stop, he piled out and squeezed off a shot. Immediately down went a full-size javelina.

As we walked toward it, he said, "I sure hope it's a boar. I want a boar in the worst way." I told him it was almost impossible to distinguish between a boar and a sow while they were alive, but generally the males were bigger in body than the females. Upon reaching the javelina and closely inspecting it, Chuck realized he had taken a sow. "I told you I want a boar!" said he as though I had had anything to do with his slam-bang Clint Eastwood technique. We started packing the little porker back to the pickup, and, after the field dressing chore was completed and he and I were both smelling like what he had just taken, plus a year's supply of fleas, I reminded him that the bag limit was two per year and that he had one more chance.

About a half mile down the road we spotted a small herd of the peccaries munching on cactus. "This time look 'em over good before you shoot. Try to pick out the biggest in the bunch." Chuck responded by cocking the hammer on the Contender and squeezing a shot. I watched as the biggest in the herd folded. After a few "Atta boy's!" we made our way to the javelina, which had fallen in the center of what seemed like one huge clump of cactus with each pad having more than its full compliment of spines, large and small. Chuck was well ahead of me and reached the javelina before I did. "Did you get a boar this time?" asked I. "Don't know yet," came the reply.

Just then I noticed Chuck raise his foot and nudge the animal's tail end, and, as the toe of his boot touched the "dead" javelina, it resurrected. With one fluid motion the javelina was up, angry as a nest of hornets. Its eyes glowed red as it made a swipe at Chuck's boot, started popping its teeth, and woofing. My friend was, at this point, in full retreat, with the mad javelina nipping at his heals. The javelina was woofing, and Chuck was screaming and hollering. It sounded as though the pair had just blasted through the gates of Hades. My normally not-so-quick friend was moving with the grace and speed of a world class hurdler, clearing one cactus after another in his attempt to get away from the enraged porker. Right at his heels was the javelina, making its last stand and promising to take "no prisoners" as it left this world for pig heaven.

"Shoot the damn thing!" hollered my compadre.

"You shoot him!" I hollered back. Making a hasty retreat, I shouted at him: "You got the pistol."

"Ain't got any bullets left! You do something!"

Pads of prickly pear were flying in every direction as Chuck ran in an ever widening circle to escape the razor-sharp teeth of the porker. "Then run!" I hollered from the safety of the back of the pickup.   As Chuck came charging my direction, I could see his eyes glaring at me, smoldering in furious hate.   You see, I was laughing so hard that I could hardly breathe and my sides felt as though they would burst. Chuck, on the other hand, had really lost his sense of humor. Behind him the javelina was slowing, which had won the battle but was about to lose the war.   So as I sat there laughing like a fool, I had two pairs of beady, red-rimmed eyes glaring daggers at me.   Panting with exertion, my compadre hissed, "You had better laugh now, because when I send you a bill for clearing two acres of prickly pear you'll . . . see."   Really, some people have no sense of humor!

His turn to laugh came a couple of days later when another javelina put me up a mesquite tree not especially designed to support a 230-pound hunter laden with handguns and cameras.   I was doing fine until he threw the bunch of mad javelinas an axe!

Because the javelina can be hunted in South Texas year around, it is an ideal game animal for entertaining magazine editors and their guests.   These guests, who are usually representatives of ad agencies, most often come from the northern climes, and, from my experience their only exposure to javelina has been the aforementioned western pulps.   When one of my favorite editors called to ask if he could bring someone with him for our annual javelina hunt, I was totally agreeable.

The pair arrived in style.   The editor was dressed in jeans, shirt, hat, and boots.   The guest was a sight to behold: slick shiny britches, silk shirt, and patent leather shoes with slick leather soles.   To complete this interesting fashion statement, on his head he wore a purple version of an Indiana Jones hat and strapped on his hip, movie-western style, was a revolver, complete with a tie-down for quick-draw action.   Being a real-quick study, I could tell at a glance that this dude had never been in the Southwest desert country hunting javelina.

Hastily I explained our game plan of using a call to sound like a javelina in trouble.   "With any luck," I told them, "we would attract the resident herd of javelinas.   Then if all went right, the javelinas should come charging, with their teeth a'popping and their hackles on end.   They would charge in close, grunting and woofing, but likely not complete the charge.

THE TROUBLE WITH JAVELINAS

It can get pretty western with the javelina at such close quarters, so let's stand with our backs together—that way we can protect all sides." The editor snickered a bit, knowing what could happen. Being in close quarters with a herd of teeth popping, mad javelina can turn anyone's knees to tortilla dough. The stranger did not know what to expect, but with a six shot, .44 Magnum revolver strapped to his side and his hand at ready, he did not seem too concerned. We chose a likely looking spot and waited.

Just as the sun fell below the blue western hills, I pulled out my call and started blowing with all my might and trying to make as much racket as possible. Obviously I was better than I thought because, before I could draw a second breath, javelina started coming out of the brush from three different sides. Their teeth were popping, making the quiet desert scene sound just like a Cinco de Mayo celebration. The ensuing cacophony was soon complemented by woofing and squealing as more and more javelina came out of the brush and ran in our direction. We were quite quickly in a maelstrom of sound.

One old boar made a four-foot distance pass at the stranger. Quicker than the last gunfighter, he drew the .44 Mag and fired, missing the pig by a good five feet. The ear-tattered, battle-scarred old peccary turned to retreat. Right behind him went the stranger, shooting and hollering. The editor and I looked in amazement at each other as they disappeared in the brush. All else was forgotten as we intently listened to the peccary pursuit. Suddenly the direction of the teeth popping, woofing, human hollering, and sounds of .44 Mag shots changed. Then from out of the brush ran the stranger. Right on his heels was a mad javelina. They circled our position and then again disappeared into the brush. Moments later here the pair came into sight again, the javelina gaining with each step. The stranger begged for help.

But by then the editor and I were laughing too hard to help. As they circled our position once again, we watched as the stranger sailed into the top of a nearby juniper, safe and out of harm's way. The enraged javelina skidded to a halt at the base of the tree and began savagely biting the bark on the trunk. With the stranger safely treed and with tears streaming from our eyes in laughter, the editor and I almost

[67]

fell from our respective perch in a nearby oak, where we had perched ourselves in self-defense. Five minutes later, with a mere flicker of daylight remaining, the old warrior grew tired of the game and departed unscathed to rejoin his herd.

THE TROUBLE WITH JAVELINAS

It took considerable coaxing to convince the stranger it was safe to come back to earth. Finally he started his descent. Just as the stranger's left foot touched the ground, the editor slapped the stranger's leg and "woofed." Back up the tree in record time went the stranger. Our laughter subsided only after he reloaded the revolver and threatened to shoot the next one of us who snickered or even cracked a smile.

Javelina have not always locally been considered game animals, especially on some of the larger ranches just above the Rio Grande. But they have long been a topic of hunting tales and tales of daring-do, especially around a campfire when the blue blaze of mesquite coals would gradually turn to ashes. I recall one such session on a cool December night. And with your indulgence, I would like to lay one of those tales on you, true though it is.

On a large ranch down south, javelina were making a genuine nuisance of themselves, especially by killing dogs. Each time the rancher worked cattle in one particular pasture, javelina would maim and/or kill his highly trained cowdogs. When his own attempts at ridding the area of javelina failed, he decided to hire a couple of professional javelina hunters. After a few days the hunters, Clem and Lum, had dispatched several javelina, but one bad herd remained. This was a particularly bad bunch, for their ferocity knew no bounds.

These wild pigs had nearly cut to ribbons all of Clem and Lum's dogs. Each time the dogs would bay the javelinas in a particularly dense whitebrush thicket, the pair would lose dogs. The rogue javelina herd would head for the thicket as soon as they heard the first dog bark. Once inside the dense thicket where the dogs could not easily escape, the javelinas would do their dastardly deed. It appeared for a while that the javelina herd would come out the winner, after Clem and Lum had lost most of their hounds.

At that point the pair retrenched and devised a plan.

PEAR FLAT PHILOSOPHIES

They decided they would record barking dogs on a tape recorder, then have a friend play the recording on a loudspeaker near the thicket. Beforehand the hunters would position themselves high in the only mesquite tree that grew in the thicket. Then, when the dog-killers made their way into the thicket, the pair would be ready. As evening approached, their friend turned on the tape of the barking dogs. Immediately the whitebrush thicket filled with javelina milling around in preparation for the ambush.

The primary shooter, a bit on the heavy side, started crawling out on the limb that overlooked the densest part of the thicket in order to see better. With his pump shotgun loaded and the plug removed, the hunter crept farther out on the limb. Beneath him the javelinas were milling and raising a genuine ruckus, primed to the teeth to attack on the instant. Hoping to get several pigs with one shot, ol' Clem crawled a bit farther out on the limb. Just as he got himself in position over the top of the herd and just as the sun sank into the western bed of thorns, so did Clem.

The limb on which Clem was perched starting breaking. According to witnesses, Clem fired that seven-shot pump shotgun making it sound like a fully automatic weapon as he headed toward the ground and into the herd of mad javelina. Lum meanwhile was trying to figure out what to do, but the fire coming from the end of the barrel of Clem's pump-turned-automatic blinded any help that might have been forthcoming. Lum, fearing for the safety of his old friend, held his fire; fearing for his own safety, Lum held on to the mesquite tree for dear life. When the smoke cleared, the only thing injured was Clem's pride and most of the nearby vegetation, which had been cleared by the shotgun fire and the hastily retreating javelinas.

As for Clem . . . the story ended on a sad note. The last anyone heard of Clem, he had moved up north. It seems he made it as far north as Duluth, Minnesota, before someone stopped to ask him what that strange thing was tied to his radio aerial. Clem figured if he went far enough north to where people had no idea what a tortilla was, there were not going to be anymore javelina either!

The Easy Way to Become an Expert Turkey Hunter

The true-to-the-feather-and-spur turkey hunter takes great pride in his or her calling abilities. And rightfully so, for the ability to duplicate the sounds of a turkey and learn the turkey's various vocabulary takes a great amount of time and practice. True, there are a few calls that have been simplified like some of the spring and push button boxes, but such are generally the tools of a rank amateur. The serious turkey hunter would not consider using such a contraption and would rely only upon his box calls, some of the friction-type slate calls, and the diaphragm. Some even more dedicated individuals will rely only on their own vocal chords. Throughout the past it has been my pleasure to have shared "quality turkey time" with such great callers as Eddie Salter, Wayne Carlton, Ray Eye, and Wayne Fears.

It was also my pleasure to have had a brief encounter with a person from the swamps of Louisiana. Beaudreaux Semineaux, pronounced Bow-dro (first name) Sim-in-no (last name) was his name, but his friends just called him B.S. for short. Well it truly was my pleasure to meet up with B.S., for it was he who taught me quite a few turkey-hunting tricks. B.S. came along when I most needed him—after I first started calling. Getting started was no fun, and I was having a great deal of trouble. His method and call, which used two unshelled ears of corn, were unique. According to him, the technique was simple, cheap, required very little practice, was sure fire, but required some patience.

"Day ain't nuttin tooo dis toy-keee callin'. Dem peoples dat sells dem cahls, woooooo, dey wants yeh to tinks dem toykees is smottt. Me frand, yeh lisstens to ol' Beaudreaux. Me, I tells yeh de trooth. Wooooooo, me I tells yeh, I hat shots menny o' dem toy-kees! Alls yeh needs is two ah dem airs (ears) o'connn (corn). Den walks tru dem hollahs en rubs dem two airs o' connn togetta. Naw if'n yeh doooes hit rat, day will beee sum o' dem coynels dat fallls off. Keeps on ah dooing hit, as yeh valks. Den wenns de lahst o' dem coynels iz gahn, keeps dem conn cobs encasin yeh havin ahmerginceee cos yeh dun ett too mennnee o' dem blackbarries. Den jist sitts rat dawn 'n waits faw dem toy-kees. Day'll bee-alawn derectly. Woooooo, dem toy-kees dey dairly lubbbs dem coynels of conn. Bast toy-keee cahl day iz!"

With the experience of B.S. behind me, I set out to become the best turkey caller possible—albeit using more conventional methods. So I started practicing. Now, my wife is generally a patient person, but her initial reaction to my in-house calling practice sessions was to threaten me with her broom, and my wife wields a mean broom, let me tell you. You ever tried practicing on a turkey call while someone is chasing you with a broom? To quote my erstwhile acquaintance B.S., "Woooooooo, tain't ezeee!" From there she progressed to, "Can't you go outside to make those horrible noises?" Not wanting to be beaten to a pulp by my normally mild-mannered wife, I complied, but almost immediately I heard, "Get back in this house! What will the neighbors think!"

Despite my critics, I persisted. Each year as spring turkey season approaches, the various calls are dragged out and the practice begins. And through those years I have added considerably to my collection of turkey hunting necessities, not only in calls but also with special camouflage, audio and video tapes, decoys, and several new and definitely necessary shotguns. To really get into the mood of practicing my calling, I put on my full compliment of camouflage clothing—right down to my facemask and gloves. All this is to the delight of my wife and two daughters. They smile, but deep down I know they are just humoring me . . . when what they are really thinking is, "Dad's going to practice his turkey calls again. Quick . . . turn up the stereo!" The neighbors are more honest—they simply stare and snicker. Whether loved ones or friends, all who live around me have learned over the years to expect the unexpected!

For the best results when practicing, I like to set up in the family room. That way the entire family, their guests, and

AN EXPERT TURKEY HUNTER

even the family cat can get the full benefit of my expertise. Practicing this way, it is simply amazing how good I have become and how well all that practice has paid off. Sometimes, however, I get threatened with bodily harm. The cat sometimes yowls and tries to sharpen his claws on my legs, which have been cleverly disguised as springtime vegetation. Sometimes those closest to me would even resort to psychological warfare by telling me that even a turkey in dire distress would never consider making a sound similar to those issuing forth from me. I'm a wildlife biologist and hunter, I'm tough, and I can take verbal abuse—I'd be the last to admit to sensitive feelings. With all my practicing, things began to change considerably. These days I follow the same routine, but the reception is quite different. Now I get compliments:

"My goodness dear, you really do sound like a turkey!"

"Wow Dad, you really should be able to dupe ol' wistbroom this year. I'll bet you're one of the best turkey callers in the whole world!"

"Why Dear, you sound so good I don't think you even need to practice any more!"

You see what I mean? With a little effort and practice, you too can become one of the top turkey callers of the ages. In time even your worst critics will applaud. As for actually getting those gobblers to come to your call . . . well, that's another story. . . .

Peach Tree Turkey Calls

One of the greatest thrills in hunting is to attract an animal by imitating its own sounds and vocalizations, or in the case of predators the sounds of their prey. Doing this without the aid of electronic calling devices or for that matter any man-made contraptions, at least to me, seems to add to the total experience. Always looking for ways to learn about turkey-hunting techniques, it was with pleasure I received a letter from a Mr. Weldon Walker, a gentleman from Harper, Texas. Mr. Walker had read an article I had written about calling and hunting turkeys. His letter was in response to my article:

"Dear Larry:

I have never seen anything in print about calling wild turkeys with a leaf. Growing up as a teenager in the Texas Hill Country shortly after World War I, I called up my first gobbler with a peach tree leaf. I am sure other leaves will work, but peach leaves seemed to be the favorite in our part of the country. I know it was the preferred leaf for calling with my father and older brothers. I have talked to quite a few of the area's hunters, some in their forties and fifties, about using peach leaves for turkey calls, but they have never heard of this method. I hope it isn't becoming a lost art! To me it is sort of like hunting with a bow and arrow. It is sporting and challenging!

Sincerely,

Weldon Walker"

Now as a writer it always makes you feel good to get a letter from someone who reads your stuff—at least you know someone is reading it before they use the paper to start the fire in the fireplace or stove. Mr. Walker's letter struck a chord, and I set out to learn more about calling turkeys with leaves and especially peach leaves. After about a week's worth of research, I sat down and wrote the following letter of reply.

"Dear Mr. Walker:
Thank you for taking the time to write. As a turkey hunter who fits in between the forty- to fifty-year old bracket, I must admit I have never heard of calling turkeys using a peach leaf. But I am anxious to learn and have been trying. Back in the early 1950s my maternal grandfather had a bunch of domestic turkeys running around his place down on Cummins Creek. He taught me to make a few sounds on a new green briar leaf that somewhat resembled the sounds a turkey makes. Unfortunately the area where I grew up did not have any wild turkeys at the time. But by blowing across the leaf, best as I now remember, we did get the domestic gobblers to answer us when they were in the bottoms. Last year I tried using a briar leaf to duplicate the sounds I was taught to make those many years ago. The sounds I made in no way resembled the yelp of a turkey hen, but, after making that sound for a while, two turkey buzzards circled overhead.

"Recently I was visiting J. Wayne Fears from Alabama, who among other things is a turkey hunter *extraordinaire*. Wayne has written many articles about turkey hunting as well as several books on the subject. Wayne, his wife, Sherry, and I get together whenever possible to hunt, visit, and enjoy a bit of peach nectar. One of the things we discussed recently dealt with turkey hunting and the various types of calls used. When I asked him about calling gobblers with a leaf, he told me his father, an Alabama backwoodsman, had taught him to call turkeys with several kinds of leaves when he was a youngster. But he had never used a peach leaf.

"During our discussion on turkey hunting, we lamented over the fact that turkey hunting is seemingly going into the high-tech age. Today a turkey hunter is not happy unless he has four or five kinds of calls, everything from an owl hooter, a gobble box, a cheek full of diaphragms, a multitude of various box, to slate and friction calls. We wondered whatever happened to using turkey wing bone calls, or even slate or cedar

PEACH TREE TURKEY CALLS

striker calls housed in a turtle shell. I guess we can all blame that on progress. Or maybe it is simply we American hunters like to be surrounded with gadgets, hoping they will give us an edge over the wise old gobblers. I suppose with turkeys it sure does not hurt to have everything you can stacked in your favor and against the old longbeards.

"After I got your letter I made a trip to our backyard. My wife has been nurturing three peach trees for several years, of which she is justifiably proud. Talk about an ideal setup: I have all the peach leaves I need to practice calling turkeys, and to make it even better my wife and daughters are away visiting grandparents. Through your encouragement I decided to learn how to make turkey sounds with peach leaves, no matter to what extent I had to go.

"A couple of days into the project, I was no more adept at making turkey sounds with a peach leaf than when I started. I have tried every method imaginable to use the leaf. Some leaves were accidentally swallowed. I guess I was inhaling when I should have been exhaling. My efforts, however, have attracted quite a bit of attention from the neighbor's dogs and cats. My next door neighbor has obviously been entertained by my efforts as well. He has spent several hours peering across my fence . . . I guess it has been to try to figure out what kind of lame-brained scheme I have come up with this time. Try as I may, the turkey leaf technique just does not seem to be working for me.

"Although saddened by my inability to perfect my technique using a peach leaf, that is really not the reason I'm writing to you at this time. Actually I have a much more serious and pressing problem and need some help. My wife and daughters are scheduled to return from their visit tomorrow, and I have got to figure out how to explain to my wife why her carefully nurtured peach trees no longer have any leaves on them. Reckon you could help me convince her we had a freak hail storm that only fell on her three peach trees? Or some strange new disease has hit selected peach trees? I intend to introduce you as a peach tree expert; do you think you can come up with any convincing ideas?

Seriously looking for help,

Larry L. Weishuhn."

Jubel, The Lonesome Dove Turkey

It is not often those of us who live in the western part of the country get to see a television show about Westerners and Southwesterners that is done correctly. All too often the major parts are played by actors and actresses who were coached how to talk like a Westerner by someone who lives in New York City. Even worse, most of the television shows that supposedly originate in Texas feature actors that talk like they have a horrible nasal condition. Equally all too often those actors know as much about horseback riding and guns as does the Queen of England's gardener.

So you can imagine how those of us west of the eastern turkey habitat felt when finally there was a show that made us feel good about ourselves. I doubt very seriously if anyone interested in television shows about the west missed seeing the miniseries "Lonesome Dove," either the first time or the rerun. To quote a fellow Texan, "That was one plum refreshing show!" What has this got to do with turkey hunting? Well, I thought you would never ask! Just sit back, relax, and allow me to tell you a tale about one of the most famous Rio Grande turkeys in history.

It actually all happened sometime back when they were first putting together the miniseries "Lonesome Dove." But much of the truth about that famous turkey did not come out until the day after the last episode of the series. That day I happened to be in Austin, Texas, taking care of some wildlife business with the Texas Parks and Wildlife Department. As a former employee of the TPWD, my travels to the Austin headquarters complex are much more enjoyable now than during the days when I worked as a wildlife biologist for the outfit. While in Austin, I wanted to visit with some of my old compadres who still draw their wages from the state. We agreed to meet in one of the local caffeine cantinas for breakfast.

While awaiting the bacon, eggs, and tortillas, we discussed some of the finer points and parts of the "Lonesome Dove" miniseries. In a booth near ours was seated a family talking about the same show.

"Dad," spoke one of the older daughters, "when that old buffalo hunter came riding up on the plains of Kansas with a turkey, where did he find it? That didn't look like any turkey country we've ever hunted! I didn't even see a tree or anything for a turkey to roost or hide in!"

Normally I would not have eavesdropped, but, since she mentioned hunting and turkeys and since she was a young lady of about thirteen, that caught my undivided attention. I was amused by her question because my wife had asked me the exact same thing. Looking over toward our table, the father recognized one of the guys at our table as a biologist with the game department, so he said to his daughter,

"Go on over and ask one of them, they're the experts."

She started our way. I picked up on what was going on and with a sweep of the hand and in my best Gus impression I said,

"Lorie darlin', drag up a stump and have a seat, I'll be more'n happy to tell you about that turkey!"

She responded by pulling up a chair and intently listening to my tale about the Lonesome Dove turkey.

"It was back in winter that I got a call from the Hat Creek outfit, headquartered at the time here in Austin. They said they needed a turkey for a movie they were gonna be a doing. Said it was gonna be called "Lonesome Dove." I thought a moment and replied, 'iffin it was gonna be about a dove, why'd they need a turkey? If it was gonna be about a turkey they oughta rename the movie Lonesome Turkey!' The man from Hat Creek replied that they were just trying to do the story how this fella from Texas, Larry McMurtry, had written it. And they needed the turkey for shooting a scene supposedly in Kansas. To which I replied, 'well, why do you want a turkey from Texas?' He responded by saying there weren't any turkeys of consequence in Kansas, so they needed a Texas turkey. Then he proceeded to tell me that they needed the turkey by a certain

JUBEL, THE LONESOME DOVE TURKEY

time and that they wanted to shoot the Kansas scene just southwest of Austin. Now, I was getting a bit confused. 'Austin, Kansas?' said I. `No,' explained he. `Austin, Texas, and could I have it on location well before daylight on the specified day?' To all of which I replied, 'Yep!'

Bad answer that 'Yep!' Therein that small word lies an adventure that would all too clearly make me understand what Cap'n Call meant when he said that the next time he gave his word to do something he'd study a mite longer before saying yes! There wasn't much of the hunting season left in which to take a turkey. And, I wanted this to be a very special old bird, not just one of your ol' everyday run-of-the-riverbottom kind. No sir, this one had to be special!

I knew there was this one old wise gobbler, living back in one of the box canyons that runs into the West Prong of the Nueces River. Weren't many turkeys back in that part of the country, but what was there was awfully smart, including one I had been trying to shoot for the last couple of years. I started calling him ol' Jubel. Named him after Jubel O'Shaunessy, a no-account old reprobate I knew on the Brazos. 'Course during the past couple of hunting seasons I called that old bird several other things when there wasn't any youngins around. Yessir! I made myself a promise I was gonna make ol' Jubel a television star, even if it might not be to his liking. Ol' Jubel was gonna be famous, seen by millions of TV viewers. Why he'd be the envy of all turkeydom!

That night I drove to the ranch, and, after the sun had sunk low to where it was a-shining on China, I walked out under the stars and spoke real loud. 'Jubel, you old thunderthroat, I promise I'm gonna make you a star!' I was to learn that Ol' Jubel must not have been too impressed with my promise of making him a genuine TV star.

The next morning just as the sun illuminated the smog and haze over old San Antonio, the future TV star gave forth a mighty gobble. To me it sounded like a challenge, just like he knew I was coming after him. The canyon where 'Ol Jubel lived was rough, so I was a little late in reaching his roosting area. His roost was in a stand of gnarled liveoaks—tough old oaks living in a country of sparse soil formed from pebbles of limestone, dead leaves, and centuries of turkey droppings.

[81]

PEAR FLAT PHILOSOPHIES

It was quite possible Jubel's ancestors had been roosting in these same oaks back during the time "Lonesome Dove" was written about. Years of avoiding predators, both four-legged and two-legged, had been bred into Jubel and his tribe.

Like a finely blown Murrano glass, these harsh conditions had tempered Jubel into something special. Not only was he worldly and smart, he had a long beard that would have done justice to Rip Van Winkle. He had a set of spurs that would have brought tears of envy from any vaquero's eyes. I wondered if that was where the long ago Spanish and Mexican cowboys had gotten their ideas for spur. Several times in the past I had watched from a distance as Jubel courted his lady friends in the spring. I suppose he was a lot like Gus, chasing the ladies of the evening. If you will pardon that expression, Ma'am.

But come fall he was much more serious about life—more reserved, kinda acting like Cap'n Call. When fall arrived, he would split off from the rest of the flock and spend the winter with only a few male companions, mostly gobblers of his same age. Only occasionally would they allow the company of a younger gobbler. Since it was late December, Jubel was spending his time trying to make a living. He was hardly thinking of the ladies, which was gonna make taking him and making him famous a whole lot harder.

During the next couple of days I challenged him time and time again with fall turkey language I had learned back when I worked for the Lone Star Outfit (sweeping my hand and pointing to the Texas Parks and Wildlife Department biologists). But ol' Jubel was much too smart for such goings on. His compadres came to investigate a few times, but not him. He stayed back in the thick brush. I gotta admit I considered taking one of them, several times. But, I'd made ol' Jubel a promise! He was gonna be a TV star whether he liked it or not! Seemed like nothing I tried worked, and time was a running out.

After several sleepless nights, I devised a plan. Since I couldn't seem to shoot him, I decided I'd catch him on the roost! So about the middle of the afternoon, I crawled into the old turkey's roost tree, covered head to toe with camouflage. I looked just like a big tree limb. I reasoned that when Jubel flew into his tree to spend the night, I'd be able to catch him quicker than a jake could catch a June bug! I admit I

JUBEL, THE LONESOME DOVE TURKEY

must have fallen asleep a few times waiting for Jubel to come to roost. I even dreamed about how things would be after I caught him.

I knew the movie makers were getting anxious. . . . By some of the bad things they had called me on the telephone, I knew they wanted the turkey real bad. And like Cap'n Call, I was about to start regretting the promise I'd made to ol' Jubel. Finally just before dark, Jubel appeared under the tree and looked up suspiciously. Spying the turkey hen decoy I had set on top of my head, the old bird let out a thunderous gobble. He strutted around, fanned his tail, and again looked up at what he thought was a turkey hen. He flapped his wings. It was beginning to look like ol' Jubel was a lot more like Gus than Cap'n Call!

In less than the twitch of a steer's horn, he flew up right beside me, convinced that spring and romancing had arrived a whole lot sooner than he had expected. Much to his surprise, the big limb where he had planned to roost for the night reached over and grabbed him. Before he could realize what was happening, I had slapped my turkey hunting license tag on his leg and stuck him in a sack . . . er . . . ah . . . make that a bag! This, of course, made my maneuver completely legal of rendering a turkey to bag.

With that I jumped from the tree and pulled out for Austin to make the early morning camera call. I felt good and at peace with the world. A promise had been kept! "Lonesome Dove" had its Kansas turkey from Texas, and I had made good on my promise of making ol' Jubel a national TV star and celebrity!

So Lorie Darlin,' the next time someone asks you about how Lonesome Dove got its Kansas turkey, you can tell them the truth.

Finishing my tale, I turned around. There behind me were half the customers in the restaurant, all attentively listening to how I had come to play a small part in the production of "Lonesome Dove." Never one to waste a good audience, before they could leave I began to unfold another story. "Did I ever tell you about the time I tied an alligator across the top of my wife's new . . . ?"

Turkeys, Rattlesnakes, and Briars

Spring turkey hunting in the Old South takes on a traditional air where turkey calls, camouflage clothing, and shotguns are the tools of the trade. But that is not yet the case in many other parts of the country. . . .

In the Southwest I know a lot of people who are still not what most would consider serious turkey hunters, including many Texas rancher friends. Some of them still prefer to shoot their gobblers with a turkey/varmint rifle at a couple hundred yards, while driving the pasture roads and checking on stock.

Some time ago I asked one of those Stetsoned turkey hunters, safely seated in the cab of his pickup, why he did not seriously get into turkey calling. I knew him to have a great interest in wild turkeys because of his wildlife habitat management program. His reply was simple, "rattlesnakes and chiggers!" Having side-stepped a few angry, hungry, and just-out-of-the-den rattlers, as well as having spent many hours scratching chigger bites, I could understand his line of thinking. Perhaps I should have paid closer attention to his two words . . . especially the one concerning long slithery things.

It all happened a couple of springs ago while I was hunting turkeys in Coleman County. Coleman is one of those Texas counties that has many more residents of the winged variety than of the two-legged kind. The evening before the hunt was to take place we, Harv and I, located a large flock of turkeys. With a brilliant orange sky as a backdrop, we watched several old longbeards fly to roost in the tall liveoak and pecan trees growing along the banks of the Jim Ned Creek. Outcroppings of limestone told of the region's past history, when many thousands of years ago this area had been the bottom of an ancient sea. Small caves, cracks, and crevices in the limestone now provided homes for a variety of smaller wildlife, including snakes. Even at a distance, the banks of the creek bottom looked "snaky."

That night my friend and sometimes-hunting-partner, known to be a bit "snaky" himself on occasion, made plans for the coming morning's hunt. Our plan was to get as close as possible in the darkness of the predawn to set up and then to call a gobbler from his roost. Sounded good to me!

As we stopped the pickup that morning, I had a feeling of doom. It was one of those unexplained feelings you sometimes get, and it hit me right in the pit of my stomach. I should have heeded the warning because it was the same feeling I had gotten many years earlier when a couple of cousins and I got in trouble because we ate too many peaches "stolen" from a neighbor's tree. Somehow a good scolding or trip behind the woodshed would have been much better than the price we paid for eating all those tasty morsels. That same feeling hung in my stomach as we got out of the pickup and headed into the darkness. We didn't want to spook the turkeys, so we decided to approach the roost in total darkness and not to use a flashlight.

That was our first mistake! It was dark! I mean to tell you it was as dark as the inside of a gobbler's gizzard. As we shambled forward, we had to feel our way through the darkness, carefully placing one foot in front of the other. Harv, who was in the lead, got battered the most when he would occasionally trip over a rock or walk into a barbed-wire fence. Up until that time I did not realize he was a stoic. Only rarely did he even grunt. In spite of the roughness of the terrain and the pitch-black that surrounded us, we made pretty fair progress . . . except when we nearly fell off of a bluff that bordered the creek bottom.

If one believed in omens, then the eastern sky prophesied doom, for there was not so much as a hint that we'd ever see another day! Ever since leaving the pickup, I had been listening for the slightest sound that might even remotely resemble the slithering of a snake. I knew from past experience that this area of Texas not only held the state's largest wild turkey population, but it also had more than its share of rattlesnakes. The warm weather of early spring with its full sunny days was just the perfect inducement for every slithery reptile for miles around to ooze out of their dens and prowl about for food.

Both Harv and I must have had the same thought because, when we suddenly heard the unmistakable steady buzz of a rattler, we both froze on the spot. It was close, and it was big and mean—other than that we didn't need to be introduced on a first-name basis. We both stood like statues, trying to determine exactly where the snake was in the pitch black darkness. Harv must have believed the snake was right in front of him because he jumped backward and, in so doing, passed me. At the same time I felt something strike my leg, just above my mid-calf high boots. Immediately I felt a sharp pain. I panicked and started jumping and hollering. To make matters worse, it felt as if the rattler was hanging on to me and my pants leg. With that awful thought, I started a violent kicking match, trying to dislodge the snake.

The more I kicked, the more it swung around my leg, writhing and striking the other leg as well. The more I hollered for help and relief, the more Harv hollered. In the distance I vaguely remember the turkeys started gobbling as well. I did not know what to do! Finally in pure panic, I started running hoping to dislodge the snake. But in dogged determination, the snake held on no matter what I did. I remembered thinking if only we had brought a flashlight, at least then I could see to shoot the snake from my leg.

I screamed for Harv to please shoot the snake. Thank goodness he did not, because in our state of shock he would have likely shot my leg completely off. The more I kicked the more the snake seemed to be striking me. I knew I was history. About five seconds into my ordeal, although it seemed like five eternities, Harv regained a bit of sanity. He produced a small box of matches and started striking them one by one and throwing them at my feet.

Afraid to look down I begged, "Shoot it, shoot it!" After about the fifth or sixth match, Harv burst out laughing. I was ready to kill him! There I was dying of a rattlesnake bite and there he was doubled over, rolling on the ground laughing. Finally I had the courage to look down at my leg, since the violent movement of the snake had stopped. There entangled in my pants leg was a three-foot piece of briar.

PEAR FLAT PHILOSOPHIES

Maybe shooting a gobbler from the safety of a pickup is not such a bad idea after all!

Bubba Eugene

"Hey, Bro, Bubba Eugene heah, watts hapmin?" queried the voice on the telephone. Before I could answer, the voice continued, "Yah gotny messkeet wood chopped fah me? I's bout dun used allus I's takin' witt me lass time. Wears ya beena keepin yoursself? My podnah 'n me, wee's been bizzy. Ah tells you 'bout hit sum later." Getting serious, Bubba quickly changed his voice to: "The mini-round man and I been on the road, been working on some lion and bear cases dealing with caged hunts. Where you been?"

No sooner had we visited but a little, than quickly the voice on the phone would say, "Gotta go, our man just finished his coffee and he's on the move. Looks like he going to cross over into Colorado. Call you in a few days after we get the paperwork done on this one."

Back in those days I never really knew who my friend was going to be whenever the phone rang. Normally if he was on the road on a case he was Bubba Eugene, but, if he was working an operation that dealt with the sale of illegal eagle feathers, the call might be from Joe Two Eagles. Bubba Eugene, more properly Bubba Eugene Ledbetter, was one of several aliases of a gentleman I met quite a number of years ago on a ridge in southern New Mexico's Lincoln National Forest.

While on our hunting trip in New Mexico, the local game wardens had heard there were several Texas biologists hunting in the area and out of courtesy sent an invitation for us to stop by the game department cabin for some coffee. At the time Ron Porter, A.K.A. Bubba Eugene, was the district warden for the Carlsbad area. In time he went on to become what we often referred to as the department's "Pinkerton Agent."

PEAR FLAT PHILOSOPHIES

Whenever there was a covert operation dealing with illegal wildlife sales, Bubba Eugene was called in.

One such operation dealt with the sale of rare, threatened, endangered, and protected reptiles, primarily snakes. When he called, "Watts hapmin Bro? Gotny 'vice bout hanlin' snakes? I's don't liekum!" Switching voices and personalities on me again, he continued, "You ain't going to believe this. We just filed charges against a couple for bringing in endangered snakes out of Mexico. You'll never guess how they were transporting them across the border."

Before I could answer, he continued, "We got several tips about the pair telling us that they would bring in any kind of snake you wanted—from some of the endangered mild snakes to black mambas. So I set up a buy. The couple shows up in a van. So naturally we suspected they were somehow using the van to smuggle the snakes in to the country; we thought they possibly had a secret compartment in the van. Wrong! I noticed when we met that the woman was pretty well endowed for not being any taller than she was. As we talked, I guess I was staring somewhat. That's when I noticed it seemed her bosoms were moving, squirming a bit. `Odd,' I remember saying to myself. Wanna guess how they were smuggling in the snakes? All I can say is that the woman liked snakes a whole lot better than I did!"

In time Porter went on to become the regional supervisor for the department's southeast sector, a position he held until he retired. As is typical of that portion of New Mexico, extended droughts are not uncommon. During one of those long dry spells, the hills and mountains were extremely dry, and quite a few bear moved to the lower country and into the towns and city for food and drink. It was during one of those spells Porter called, laughing.

"We been having bear problems in towns. Got a call from one of my district officers who said he would have a local citizen call me. Just got off the phone with the guy. Thought you might be interested since you enjoy bear."

According to Ron, the call went something like this. . . . "Kay man, ju got one of jour bears here at my casa. Ju come get him, rapido!"

BUBBA EUGENE

"Yes sir. Where is the bear now, and what is he doing?" asked Porter.

"Kay man, hee's on the back of my peecup truck. Kay man, my bro's and me were going to the park to drink a little Cerveza. But de bear he is eating up all our *comida* and starting to drink our Cerveza. Kay man, ju come gets dis bear!"

By this time I know that Porter must have been snickering just a little, but still he replied, "Yes sir, he's probably just hungry and thirsty. I'll send one of our units with a tranquilizer gun."

"Kay man, the bear hee's about to drink all our beers. What should we do?" queried the man with the beer-drinking bear on the back of his pickup truck.

PEAR FLAT PHILOSOPHIES

Bubba Eugene thought for a minute, then replied: "Sir, I suggest you send someone to the store to buy more beer. A half-drunk bear is a whole lot more dangerous than one totally drunk!"

It is suspected that it was Bubba Eugene who sent in a request to the state office that year requesting a stocking of "walking catfish" for the southeastern sector. The reason given on the cut-and-dry government form was that, even if all the water holes dried up, all would not be lost and the area's citizens could continue fishing!

Through the years Ron and I have developed a friendship that transcends the 500 miles that normally separates us. Few weeks go by where we do not spend our total monthly phone budget visiting with each other. Ron has the unique second sense to call when I really need a friend to talk to about a problem. I sometimes think he knows more about what I am and what I am doing than I do. Each year we arrange to make at least a couple of hunts together, be it for mule deer, elk, pronghorn antelope, white-tailed deer, wild hogs, or javelina. Those hunts are always highly successful, even if we do not squeeze the trigger. While together there are times we talk up a storm and also times when we might not say a word while staring into the last glowing embers of the campfire. In those instances there is no need to speak, we simply appreciate each other's company. Partners like him are hard to find!

Me and Bubba

Jay Verzuh is a western Colorado outfitter who operates his extremely well-run and successful business under the name of Colorado Elite. Since our first hunt together, he and I have been friends. Unfortunately, we do not get to see each other as much as we would like. But then too, that is probably fortunate for both of us. I first met Jay under some interesting circumstances. The following is our first contact and correspondence with each other.

Mr. Jay Verzuh
Grand Junction, Colorado

"Dear Mr. Verzuh:
I am truly looking forward to our mule deer hunt together in November as arranged by Ms. Sherry Fears. I have longed to hunt mule deer in Colorado for quite some time. I must, however, explain a little about myself so you can see to it that my hunt will be both enjoyable and successful. I weigh 475 pounds and stand 5' ½" tall. (In truth, at the time I weighed 220 pounds and stood 6'3" tall and was in reasonably good health and condition.) Although I am not in tip-top shape, I can reasonably walk from the table to the closest pickup without getting winded. But I am not a mountain climber. I do not have a very good sense of direction and have the tendency to get lost when I get too far from the hunting vehicle. With much exertion, my glasses get fogged up. Unfortunately without them I am blind as a bat. My doctors tell me I have a serious heart condition and have to be extremely careful about not overtaxing myself.

PEAR FLAT PHILOSOPHIES

"Too, I have an aversion to loud noises and recoil, therefore I shoot only .22 caliber rifles. My greatest pleasures of being in a hunting camp are consuming great volumes of various libations with a high percentage alcohol base and, quite frankly, eating. Nothing makes me as hungry as being in a hunting camp. I am truly looking forward to a successful hunt with you. Ms. Fears assured me if anyone could help me break my twenty-year slump on mule deer, it would be you!

Respectfully,

Larry L. Weishuhn."

I sent this letter to Mr. Verzuh after I received a list of what to take on the hunt and the camp rules. Jay's rules included: The hunter is required to shoot at least a .24-caliber rifle, the hunter must be in top physical condition to hunt, and anyone under the influence of alcohol would immediately be asked to leave camp. So imagine, if you will, being a conscientious outfitter in Colorado and receiving a letter such as the one sent to Jay Verzuh. I later learned that Jay, upon receiving my letter, couldn't make up his mind whether it was a joke or not. His reply came a couple of weeks later:

"Dear Larry:

Received your letter last week while we were still in the mountains, scouting. I appreciate the "personal" data provided, as it will allow me to match you with a guide who will make your hunt much more enjoyable. I have decided to have Bubba be your personal guide. He is approximately ten pounds lighter than you, and has a serious aversion to anything other than flat land and vehicles. His eyesight is about par with yours, so he also doesn' t dare getting beyond fifty yards of the pickup without getting seriously lost.

"As far as your loud noise problems and heart condition—not to worry. Bubba hasn't found a deer in the past five years. The best news is that during the off-season Bubba drives a beer truck and always has an ample supply of "hootch," which has a mysterious way of falling from the delivery truck. All in all, it should be a dream trip for you. You won't have to worry about missing or dragging a deer or overtaxing your body. This

ME AND BUBBA

will allow you a lot of time to work up many "stories" to write up when you return. See you soon.

Aiming to please, sincerely,

Jay Verzuh."

Bear in mind, Jay and I had not yet met in person up to this point and never had seen each other, except possibly in magazine photos. I arrived at the Grand Junction Airport full of expectation for a good laugh once I got to the hunting camp. The Fears met me at the airport, helped me buy the licenses, and then drove me to Jay's home. As we drove up to Jay's front yard, filled with fellow hunters and guides, one individual immediately caught my attention: There in the middle of the group stood, shall we say, a rather portly gentleman, weighing in at about 435 pounds and wearing an orange cap with a beer insignia on the front. My immediate thoughts were . . . you guessed it, h-e-r-e-'s Bubba.

I paid very little attention to the names of the people I was introduced to outside of Jay, who had more than one twinkle in his eye. I introduced myself. "Pleasure to meet you," was all Jay said. Walking over to the big guy with the beer cap, I remember thinking. . . . "My goodness, now you've really done it this time, Weishuhn! This'll teach you to be smart-alecky! This guy's probably got hootch stored all over the place, and you hardly ever drink the stuff. More than likely, you won't ever get close enough to even see a mule deer this entire trip!"

Walking closer to the gentleman, I started to say something like, "Well . . . well, you must be the legendary Bubba," but then hesitated. A broad smile swept across the large man's face and he stuck out his hand. "Hello, my name is. . . ."

I listened more intently than I thought earthly possible. Surely this had to be Bubba. Jay Verzuh stood near the mountain of the man, grinning and eyes a-twinkling. Both Wayne and Sherry moved closer, as they had seen both my and Jay's letter. ". . . Dave, and I'm one of Jay's hunters from Wisconsin," finished my new-found friend.

Late that evening Jay was still laughing as we settled into his camp. In between chuckles, he said, "Well at least your

[95]

color has returned. You should have seen the look on your face when you stepped out of the car." This was followed by another round of knee-slapping laughing. As he got up and walked out the door, he stopped, looked my way, grinned and said, "Oh by the way, the real Bubba will be here in about an hour, he probably got lost again. . . . ."

Colorado Cliffhanger

It was a no-win situation. In an effort to drop down to where a huge nontypical mule deer buck was reported to be, I had foolishly tried to climb down a rimrock where the only hand-holds were thin cracks in the rock facing. My right hand clutched the stock of my new Remington Mountain Rifle, chambered in .280 Remington. Foolishly I had forgotten the sling in camp. The fingers of my left hand were firmly wedged in a thin crack in the rock facing. So there I hung with my hand stuck in the crack, my right hand holding on to my rifle, and my feet dangling about four feet above anything solid . . . solid that is if you could call a near-perpendicular slope of shale and small gravel anything solid.

For a moment my thoughts drifted to an ordeal that happened to a past-hunting companion of mine while he was on a sheep hunt. He had fallen several hundred feet but had survived and recovered after many months in a hospital. Today he makes his living writing and singing songs and goes by the nickname of Bocephus. Not possessing much of a singing voice or talent for writing songs, I wondered what the future would hold for me . . . that is, if I survived the fall. Right now the future looked pretty bleak.

As is often the case when one gets into a serious life-threatening situation, a black humor emerges. I could see the headlines back in our hometown paper . . . "Noted Area Wildlife Biologist and Part-time Scribe Found Hanging From a Colorado Cliff."

Hanging there with little else to do, I found myself recalling a somewhat similar incident I had gotten myself into several years ago, again while hunting trophy mule deer in the Colorado high country. On that occasion my brother, Glenn, and I spent the better part of a day working our way to the top of a rimrock, thinking it the edge of a huge flat top mesa, which would be ideal country for big mule deer bucks. After hours of slipping, sliding, and crawling, we were within an arm's reach of the crest. With tremendous effort, I pulled my tired and sore body to the top and swung my legs and torso up over the edge. As the momentum of the swing pushed my body upward, I found to my horror that I had thrown myself completely over the mountaintop and was nearly off of the other side of the mountain. The huge mesa we had spent tremendous effort to attain was no more than six inches wide on top. Exasperated, embarrassed, and bone tired, I sat hugging my knees and telling myself how lucky I had been. Had I released my death-grip on the thin sliver of real estate, I would have rolled several hundred yards down the opposite slope.

Meanwhile back in southeastern Colorado, there I was still hanging on this other small sliver of real estate. This was not necessarily out of desire but born of the fact that my hand was stuck, and I could not let go. For a while I considered dropping the rifle and trying to use my right hand to pull my way up, hoping somehow and in some way that that would release my stuck left hand. But I took one look at the stock and then the scope and decided otherwise. Should I survive, I reasoned, dropping it would ruin the finish and destroy the scope.

The real cause for being stuck on the side of this mountain like a human fly was a thirty-inch wide mule deer buck with long tines and deep back forks. The outfitter had scouted and seen the buck on several occasions. In confidence he told me about the deer, saying, "I haven't told anyone else about the buck because he lives in an area that is nearly inaccessible. The only way to get to him is to drop in from above. You're welcome to try, but I warn you the country is rough!" Treacherous is more like it. In spite of my present situation, I hoped the buck would not see me hanging out, as it were, and I would still have a chance at him if I could survive the fall. But first I had to worry about getting loose and surviving a treacherous four-foot drop onto loose shale on a nearly ninety-degree slope.

It all seemed hopeless. Help was several canyons away and well beyond the sound of my shouts. There was no use to even expend the energy to try. To make matters worse, two

COLORADO CLIFFHANGER

golden eagles circled above and with each glide came a little closer. If that was not enough, just below and to my left a black bear appeared—popping his jaws as if he were mad or perturbed about something. I tried desperately to chamber a round, but it was all to no avail. Twice I nearly dropped the rifle. The bear kept coming closer, and from the look in his beady dark eyes I could tell there was murder in his black heart. In a last ditch effort, I pitched the rifle above my head so I could catch it midair, grab it by the barrel, and use the stock as a club . . . thus protecting myself from the bear, I hoped.

In doing the juggling act, I dislodged my left hand, hit the loose shale rolling down the slope, and bounced off the boulders on my rapid descent like a ball in a pinball machine. I started screaming at the top of my voice just as Jerry Baker and Bret Triplett came running to my side. . . .

I awoke on the floor of the cabin, bruised from the fall out of my bed. Dazed, my backside hurting, to say nothing of my pride, I heard Jerry Baker mumble, "Do you always scream at the top of your voice and fall out of the bed the first night in hunting camp?"

Meskin Blues, Gentleman Bobs, and a Pointing Pig

If you are expecting to read about one of those tales of a classic quail hunt steeped in the great traditions of the antebellum South, well compadre, this is not written for you! Quail hunting in the Southwest is somewhat different from the plantation-style outings of hunting with frock-coated gentlemen, accompanied by horse-drawn carriages and lunches under the magnolias.

That is not to say, however, that quail hunting in the arid land of cactus and thorn cannot compete with the quality of hunting experienced on some of Georgia's finest quail plantations. Through management techniques developed in the lower coastal areas of southern Texas, some of the better managed ranches can and do produce native bobwhite quail in numbers exceeding five birds to the acre. Mention those kind of quail populations to a dyed-in-the-wool quail hunter from the Carolinas, and he will accuse you of spreading vile rumors about everything being bigger and better in Texas. But what the heck, we true Texans know that to be a fact anyway!

There are basically two kinds of quail in the Southwest where I hunt birds: gentlemen bobwhites and blue or scaled quail. The latter are sometimes referred to as "meskin blues." The meskin blue quail makes his living in the harsh, dry country of prickly pear cactus and thornbrush along the Rio Grande. Find a seemingly bare gravel ridge near the border with Mexico, and you will find a covey of blues. The meskin blue quail is no gentleman; he is an athlete. His kind take great pleasure in outrunning and outdistancing their enemies, man with a shotgun included. Most bird-dog aficionados do not like to hunt where there are blues because blues, rather than stick tight until they are flushed, at the first sight of danger take off like a blue streak! Given the opportunity, they will flat ruin a good pointer by running him into the ground.

One of the more popular ways of hunting these speed demons is called "quail hunting, safari style." This amounts to driving ranch roads in a pickup or jeep in order to spot birds. Whenever the blues are located, the truck stops, hunters jump out, and the chase begins. I have seen entire large coveys easily outdistance would-be world-class sprinters. Meskin blues have the uncanny ability to sense the exact moment when the out-of-breath hunter can go not one step more without collapsing. At that precise moment they will take wing, leaving behind the heaving, oxygen-depleted hunter mumbling bad things about the ancestry of the entire quail family. Do I shoot meskin blues on the ground and running? Unfortunately not very well, but it is certainly not for a lack of trying!

Some of the greatest quail hunts I have enjoyed occurred during the years we lived in the northwest Texas town of Abilene, while I served as a state wildlife biologist. The region always held a decent quail population, even in bad years. Unfortunately our work schedule seldom allowed us much time to hunt until late in the season, by which time it had often gotten quite cold.

One afternoon as Roy Bamberg, my fisheries counterpart, and I departed our office, we decided a quail hunt was in order, and we were going, even if . . . ah . . . ah . . . "the hot place froze over!" We did not quite count on the little-known fact the area around Abilene would be included. Roy called later that afternoon and said a friend had offered him the use of his pointer, Luke. We were all set.

At four in the morning I arose and hurriedly got dressed. But I was not quite prepared for what waited outside the front door. Had I known, I would have donned a lot more "padding" for my backside, which I might add, was the first thing to hit the ground after being greeted by a solid sheet of ice and zero-degree temperatures. I limped back into the house to call Roy to see if he wanted to reconsider, given the treacherous weather. He mumbled into the phone something about a little ice and snow never deterring the mountain men, told me to be ready, then he hung up. Now my honor as a tough mountain man was at stake, so I did as I was told and got ready. When Roy picked me up in his four-wheel drive, we got off to a fantastic start by sliding off a solid sheet of ice that covered the pavement. After that, we went cautiously, pausing occasionally to check the depth of snow in the front yard of the houses we passed.

Luke, the pointer, was not too excited about all the goings-on. He slept through most all our slipping, sliding, and maneuvering except for when he threw up all over my lap. Ridding myself of the mess was easy. No sooner had I stepped outside then it froze solid. Up until that point, Roy had me believing all the great things he had been saying about Luke, the pointer of all pointers!

Finally we pulled into the gate and got ready for the hunt. Luke the bird dog, as soon as he was released, became Luke the rabbit dog. That is when I learned even more about bird dogs and bird-dog handlers. From what I saw then and from experience on past hunts, a real bird-dog handler stands around blowing a whistle at a dog that acts totally deaf. When the handler decides the whistle is not going to work, he starts hollering and telling the entire creation within earshot about the dog's questionable ancestry.

At any rate Roy finally gave in, and Luke continued to chase rabbits and ignore us. Meanwhile we began playing hide and seek with the resident bobwhite population. Occasionally if we happened to flush a covey and drop a bird, it would disappear with a "pooof," into the knee-deep powdery snow. Then for the next several minutes, we dug through the white stuff to retrieve the bird. I looked over at Roy, but only his glasses and eyes were visible as the rest of him was covered in heavy clothing against the cold.

Being thoroughly cold by this time, I shouted at Roy: "If only we had a decent bird dog, things would certainly be easier!" I didn't understand Roy's mumbled reply, but whatever he said melted the ice that had formed on his scarf where his mouth ought to have been!

Then lo and behold, a miracle happened. Luke started running our way! As he got closer, he did a 180° turn in mid-air and locked on point in classic pointer style—including one raised front foot and tail high in the air. Roy hollered, "Now what do you think about our dog?" Personally I was impressed but unsure what Luke was pointing. Being bitterly cold and remembering Luke's previous behavior, I was still not completely convinced that this was THE pointer of all pointers. For all I knew Luke might be pointing a skunk. Nonetheless, we walked in and quail flushed, sending a spray of many tiny snowflakes skyward. It was an unbelievably beautiful sight to behold. Recovering, three shots sounded, and three gentleman bobs fell to the ground and disappeared in the mantle of white.

"Fetch!" commanded Roy. Luke took off straight toward the downed birds. Maybe I had misjudged the pointer; perhaps he simply needed to run off a bit of energy before settling down to the job of pointing and retrieving birds.

Luke was a beautiful sight bounding through the snow, and in no time at all he stuck his muzzle into the deep snow and came up with a quail. "Good dog! Heel!" hollered Roy. The pointer took a couple of steps toward us, stopped, and before we could even think, "Don't do it!" he swallowed the quail. We stared at the dog in complete astonishment—we were dumfounded! Immediately he ran to where the second quail had fallen, located it, and swallowed that one as well. At almost the same instant Luke, Roy, and I all made a mad dash to where

BLUES, BOBS, AND POINTING PIGS

the third bird had gone down. Obviously four feet are better than two in deep snow because he easily beat us to the last quail. Thereupon the mangy cur picked it up in his mouth, mouthed it a bit, looked our way as if to say, "Heh guys, I got it!" and swallowed the third quail! It became real obvious we might have been hunting the gentleman bobs, but unfortunately Luke the pointer lacked all the gentlemanly qualities.

The following season found me accepting an invitation from a distant relative I knew as Uncle Ern. Uncle Ern lived on a fair-sized ranch in some of the best quail country north of the Rio Grande. He had two passions, hunting and "messing with" hogs, wild and domestic. Somewhere in his misspent youth, he had heard hogs were smarter than dogs. It seemed

only natural to Uncle Ern if that were the case he could train a hog to point quail.

Diligently he set forth to accomplish this world-class feat. He inspected each litter produced from his crossings between domestic and wild-trapped stock. He strongly believed these crossings would produce a genetically and intellectually superior animal. After years of trial and error, Uncle Ern came up with a calico-colored gilt he thought ideal for bird training. He invested many hours of training and work, and his efforts at training "Sookie" paid off. Once Uncle Ern decided that Sookie was "polished," he started using the quail-pointing hog in his commercial bird-hunting operation. Now I have to say that many serious quail hunters laughed at Uncle Ern and his pig, Sookie. But once they went into the field that laughter turned into respect. Uncle Ern had trained Sookie well, for his quail-pointing pig pointed covey after covey of quail.

In time Sookie's reputation grew and spread. More than a few wagers were won on bets as to which could point more coveys, Sookie the bird-hunting hog or some highly trained pointer, Brittany, or German shorthair. Sookie never let Uncle Ern down, not even once.

Finally someone suggested to Uncle Ern that he ought to enter Sookie in some of the field trials for bird dogs. He agreed and Sookie shined! Unfortunately the judges disqualified her because, when she held up her tail like the rest of the pointers, she could never quite get the kink out!

Back Sliding Quail Hunter

As a hunter I have never been known for my prowess with a shotgun. Rifle and handgun, fairly passable; shotgun and wingshooting, well I am forever in the learning stages. My lack of ability with a scattergun must date back to my formative years. In those naive days, I hunted doves with a single barrel .410 shotgun given to me as a gift by my parents. Not a single dove was safe within thirty yards, that is if they lit in the old mesquite tree that grew close to our windmill and water trough. If they flew by, they were safe!

During those early 1950s water was a precious commodity, even near where I grew up on the upper reaches of the Gulf Coast prairie. The 1950s started out as the decade it would not rain. Admittedly water was a bit more available than .410 shells. So rather than possibly waste a shot at a flying target, I waited until they landed in the gnarled mesquite. As my shotgun education progressed, I learned it was not considered sporting to shoot doves while they roosted in a tree. I also found out one ate a whole lot fewer doves when trying to shoot them on the wing. No wonder the gunwriters of the time considered them such a rare delicacy, especially if they were not any better at wingshooting than I was! Shotgun shells became a bit more available as I "matured" during my years in high school, but that only lead to my missing more shots at flying doves than I previously had.

With college came new responsibilities and a bride. During our years at Texas A&M, Miss Mary and I pretty well survived on what I could shoot, trap, or catch. Once again shotgun shells demanded a premium, and I slipped back into my old ways of shooting doves sitting in a tree, preferably if I thought I could kill four or more with one shot. I started feeling the same way when it came to quail. Why shoot one on the wing when you can shoot several on the ground? After all, empty shotgun-hull soup do not a tasty or nutritious meal make! Is it amazing what plain old hunger and an empty bank account can do for a true sportsman?

After graduation and with steady employment as a wildlife biologist for the state, a few shekels found their way into my moth-lined pocket. It was then that I started down the road to becoming a true shotgun sportsman. No more shooting doves in a tree, or covey shooting quail. No sireee!

I started reading everything I could get my hands on about shotgun shooting techniques: master eyes, shot patterns, chokes, shot size, loads, and how to increase your trap and skeet scores. Why I even learned the average hunter requires four shotgun shells to bring down a single dove, and three for every quail bagged. That national average must purely please the folks at Remington, Winchester, Federal, or anywhere else that produces shotgun shells!

Several years later you can imagine my absolute pleasure when I was given an opportunity to hunt quail with Bob Brister, shooting editor of FIELD & STREAM, and Duncan Barnes, the magazine's editor. Not only was and is Bob Brister considered "Mister Shotgun," but also he had been a personal hero for years. I could hardly wait to show off all the shotgun skills I had learned from years of reading his columns and books. I could see the headlines, "Noted Wildlife Biologist and Shotgun Shooter Teaches "Mister Shotgun" and The Editor of FIELD & STREAM New Scattergun Techniques!" . . . "Bravo, Bravo! Author, Author!"

The hunt date finally arrived. That particular year the bobwhite quail on the ranch I was managing near Hebbronville were at an all-time high. There were as many quail on the ranch as there were sandburrs. Well almost as many. The morning of the hunt Jeff Waugh, master trainer of pointing quail dogs, released a couple of his pointers. They performed flaw-lessly, point after classic point. While Bob Brister, Duncan Barnes, and others shot quail, I followed along recording the event through the view finder of a camera. The shooters seldom missed. When I thought the hunt had been sufficiently photographed, I grabbed a shotgun to join in the shooting. Enthusiasm and confidence ran high!

Bobby, Son of Winston was on point, tail high in the air, left front foot raised in classic pointer fashion. I eased into the tall grass to flush the quail, shotgun half raised and ready, thumb on the safety, and finger near the trigger. With an explosion of feathers, the nearest clump of prickly pear literally erupted with birds. Gun to shoulder, cheek to stock, sight straight down the barrel, squeeze. . . . Heck, I forgot to release the safety! Mass confusion! Finally safety off. Lead one bird and not the entire covey! Jerk the trigger . . . a perfect miss! Totally embarrassed, but then remember I have a second barrel and birds are still within range. Hurry, go through same procedures for the second barrel. This time squeeze the trigger, dummy, do not jerk it! Follow through and do not flinch! Remember you are hunting with the professionals! Blam! Another miss. I watch as the shot cup floats out no less than six feet behind the shot at quail. My foot the bobwhite is a gentleman. HA! Apologize for lack of shooting ability, make lame excuse about shirt being too tight and not allowing me to get on the birds fast enough. A muffled snicker is heard from the gallery.

Next point, Bobby, Son of Winston, turns around and gives me one of those, "You're one of those kind of shotgun shooters, boy is this going to be a long day!" looks. Knowing my procedures to be flawless, I try again. Again, the results are the same: two more embarrassing misses. Oh, no! Again I make a lame excuse. Trying to inject humor into the situation, I said something about this covey probably wearing their little flack jackets. More snickers.

As Bobby, Son of Winston, quickly located and pointed another covey, I excused myself saying I would likely have many more opportunities to shoot after our guests returned to the city, then suggested Misters Brister and Barnes take the shots. I also stated the utmost importance of me checking on the progress of supper. All agreed.

Driving back to camp, I was really feeling down. I was just bidding a soul-felt adieu to all my dreams when, lo and behold, right in the middle of the road was a huge covey of bobwhites. I slammed on the brakes, automatically grabbed the twelve gauge, and in a lot less time than it takes to write about it, I had eight quail rendered to bag. In two additional shots I had greatly upped my average, eight quail with six shots. Not too bad! Who said you had to be an expert at wingshooting to eat quail? I guess it comes down to "old habits are hard to break!" That night at supper no one seemed to be able to tell the difference between wing-shot birds and ground-shot birds, not even the professionals.

Lesson of the Alligator

Few wild creatures demand as much respect as the full-grown alligator. These remnants of the age of reptiles are unbelievably strong and quick. And in the South they are likely to show up just nearly anywhere.

A few years back when the alligator was placed on the list of threatened and endangered species, it was thought there were few alligators left in southern North America. But once the word was put out that alligators were off-limits, they seemed to start coming out of the woodwork. It did not take long for them to become a nuisance in many areas, evidenced by disappearing family pets. But that is getting a bit ahead of my story.

As a youngster growing up at a time when evenings were spent on the front porch listening to stories told by my grandfather, great grandfather, and their friends rather than sitting in front of a television screen, I learned many things. One of my favorite stories at the time was how one of my great grandfathers used to catch alligators back in the latter part of the 1800s. Using a stout steel hook attached to an even stouter steel cable and a long pole, he caught quite a few 'gators. His method was simple: find an alligator den or hole (in our part of the country usually a hole normally found dug in a creek bank), attach the hook to the end of a pole, and poke the pole into the hole to taunt the 'gator into biting at the hook. Or, if that did not work, hook the 'gator anywhere you could. Pull it out of the hole and dispatch it. Neat and relatively simple. Back then the alligators were plentiful to the point of being a nuisance, and if left unchecked they took more than their share of domestic pigs and calves that wandered close to water's edge.

PEAR FLAT PHILOSOPHIES

One of my favorite stories was about Great Grandpa Frederic: After partaking of a lot of home-brewed whiskey one night, Great Grandpa Frederic decided to go alligator hunting. When the poke-the-pole-down-the-hole technique did not work, Great Grandpa decided to crawl in the hole with the alligator and bring him out all by himself. Five minutes after disappearing into the hole, accompanied by reportedly considerable cussing on Great Grandpa's part and considerable hissing and bellowing on the alligator's part, the two emerged from the hole. All this must have had a sobering effect on Great Grandpa Frederic

LESSON OF THE ALLIGATOR

because, once they both got out of the hole, Great Grandpa decided the best place for him to be at the moment was in the top of a nearby willow tree. Great Grandpa remained in the tree until daylight, and the 'gator . . . well, the 'gator moved a considerable distance down the creek. It appears that after their encounter, neither one trusted the other a bit.

So it was somewhat honestly that I came to be standing knee-deep in a cement pond on Galveston Island surrounded by alligators. Our purpose for being there was to collect some blood samples from the alligators in the park to try to determine why they were dying. Upon our arrival the vet assigned to the 'gator project and I learned the park had found a dead eight-foot long alligator the morning of our arrival. After catching and "bleeding" several of the alligators (an ordeal in itself), we prepared for our journey home. It was at this point the vet announced, "We have to take the dead alligator back to College Station with us. It'll be an ideal way to find out what had been happening!"

I looked at him as though he had just lost his mind. "Burg, do you realize we are here in my wife's brand new Volkswagen bug? If you think I'm going to put that stinking alligator in my wife's car, you aren't too smart. I'd never get the smell out. Besides there wouldn't be room in the car for you, me, and the 'gator. Forget it!"

"I'm telling you we have to take the 'gator back with us; it's that simple!" said Burg, as he stared past my shoulder at my wife's bright, shiny, new, little red Volkswagen. "I know what we'll do!" he exclaimed. "We'll tie it on top! Hey, that'll work great!"

"Burg, do you realize we are a couple hundred miles from College Station? The alligator has just been put on the endangered species list. We have to drive back right through the middle of Houston. We'll have every game warden, county officer, highway patrol, and heaven knows who else stopping us. . . . Forget it, it wouldn't be worth the hassle," I shot back.

From the determined look on the vet's face, I knew I was doomed. Even if we escaped every single officer upholding game protection laws from here to College Station, I wouldn't escape my wife when she saw what had happened to her spanking new pride-and-joy. Boy, was I doomed! Burg's face cleared, and I realized he had come up with a plan.

"Tell you what," Burg said, "we'll do it under the cover of darkness! We'll fool around here until about 1:30 or 2:00 in the morning. There'll be very little traffic, and, if anyone sees us at that hour, they won't believe their eyes anyway." Then he added, "If there is any trouble, I'll take the blame—OK?"

I finally agreed the plan MIGHT work—at least it wasn't as bad as some of the others he had dreamed up. So that night after dark we loaded the eight-foot long dead alligator on top of my wife's new red Volkswagen. We tied his head to the front bumper and most of his tail to back bumper. The last eighteen inches of the tail hung from the back bumper. At 1:15 A.M., we pulled out of the gates of the park heading north toward College Station.

Thankfully Burg was right—there was very little traffic. The drivers of those cars that passed us were either too tired to care, or they simply ran off the road from the shock of seeing an alligator moving at fifty miles an hour on a freeway. There was one minor flaw to our plan, however: We had not filled up the car with gas before tying the alligator on top. We realized, too late of course, that this small detail could turn into a huge problem. As we approached Houston, I knew we were going to have to stop for gas.

It was the late 1960s, and all the South was embroiled in racial problems. Only the week before Houston had experienced several race riots. The area we would have to drive through was where those riots had occurred. Most businesses, including gas stations, were closed after dark. Meanwhile the gas gauge was pegging "Empty."

"Burg," said I, "we have got to pull in somewhere to get gasoline, or they're going to find a dead biologist and a dead veterinarian accompanying a dead alligator, if we run out of gas and have to spend the night in this part of town." It made me weak in the knees just thinking about it.

We pulled off of the main highway and headed to the edge of a residential section. The results of the recent riots were everywhere: Trashed store fronts, burned-out buildings, and broken glass surrounded us. Forget weak knees . . . I was scared! Then up ahead I saw possible hope. It was in the form of an all-night convenience store, with a gas pump right at the front door. As we pulled in, I noticed the only people in the store and the parking lot had a considerably darker complexion than mine. Now I was really scared.

"Burg, if we don't get killed here, it's going to be a miracle. But if we don't get gasoline, we're goners for sure. I'm going to pull right up to the front door and walk in like I own the joint. You stay here with the motor running. If things go dirty, get the hell out of here. OK?" He nodded, but being from the Northwest he did not fully understand the actual danger we faced.

I stepped out of the car and walked into the store. Immediately inside the door stood four big guys, each had their hands in their pockets, and I could see the small caliber automatics they were fingering. As I walked toward the guy behind the counter, I remember saying a small prayer, "Lord, this ain't gonna be easy!"

As I stopped in front of the cash register, the big man behind it spoke, "White blood, you de fust white man evva to come into dis place after dark!" At that point I knew I was dead for sure. My thoughts drifted to my wife, infant daughter, and of all the places I still wanted to hunt. I tried to stand as straight as possible and not exhibit any fear. "You eeda real dumb or. . . ." At that point he looked past my shoulder and out the door at the little red Volkswagen with the alligator tied on top. "Dat yor alligata?"

"Yes sir!" spoke I proudly.

"White blood, if dat's yor alligata, en you catched it 'n tied him to yor cahr, you havt bound tooo be de meanest white blood evva! Wee'll hept you widt anythin you needs!"

Sometimes the Lord works in mysterious ways!

A Christmas Story

Old Charley was not quite himself. He had an extra bounce in his step, and his steel-blue eyes twinkled like a youngster's who knew a secret and could not wait to tell someone. Normally the ornery old rascal was just that, an ornery rascal. Irascible in every way, Old Charley normally reveled in being miserable and making everyone else around him feel the same way.

Charley's camp is nestled along a creek and under ancient liveoaks, which has served weary pilgrims for hundreds of years. When we arrived there, Charley was humming a song. The tune was somewhat foreign and most of us passed it off as being a ditty Charley had picked up during the days he traveled with a packtrain through the sierras of Mexico in search of gold and lost legends.

Out in the back, the old man's mule nibbled on some freshly rolled oats, not the normal meal for this beast of burden. Ol' July generally had to survive on stemy saccatone grass, which grew along the sides of the creek. Charley dearly loved the old mule, but could never see any benefit in feeding him good groceries. Many's the time we've heard old Charley say: "Why if that ornery old mule ever ate good, he'd be plum ruint! Next thing you know he'd be expecting me to carry the load!"

Around Christmas each year, we—my brother, a couple of close friends, and I—would head to Charley's Rancho de los Cuernos. For some reason the old white-tailed bucks, fattened on mesquite beans and acorns, seemed to prefer the prickly pear flats near Charley's camp over any of the surrounding country.

I had met old Charley nearly twenty-five years earlier in a cantina near Del Rio. He appeared to be down on his luck, but still stood pine-tree straight and tall, wearing a good hat and pair of boots. I had helped him home. I remember ending up spending a couple of days with him at his ranch working cattle. As I prepared to leave, he asked if I enjoyed hunting deer.

"Yes Sir!" I replied.

So it came to be that each December since then I have returned to visit Charley, to hunt deer, and to listen for hours as the old man told tales of chasing banditos down along the Rio Bravo when he was a young man.

Charley had spent quite a few years riding the river in search of smugglers, bootleggers, and bandits back in the early 1900s. Back then you did whatever you were big enough to do, and evidently Charley had been plenty big! One of Charley's favorite tales was about the night he was on patrol with a couple of compadres.

Charley and his two look-alikes had encamped on a high bank overlooking the Rio Grande, waiting in ambush for the bandits. They had been there since early afternoon—cramped, cold, and getting stiffer and stiffer as the hours passed. Just before the inky darkness of December blanketed the area, a "Blue Norther" blew in, in true blizzard fashion. As the temperature dropped to near zero and rain turned to sleet and snow, the three men on the north side of the Rio knew that to survive the night they had but one open option: to build a fire in a steep-sided canyon. They knew that such a fire would betray their presence and position, but it was that or freeze to death.

No sooner did they have a fire roaring when they heard horses approaching. The bandits reigned their mounts close to the fire, staring at the rangers across the flames. Neither side knew what would happen next. Finally one, obviously the leader of the band, spoke in broken English: *"Amigo, the noche is muy frio.* Tonight we warm by the fire; we fight in the *mañana,* no?"

A short time later the bandits and the rangers lay beside a much larger fire and spoke of the old days. When the graying dawn foretold of the coming of daylight, the bandits and the rangers parted company. The shootout occurred a few hours later.

Old Charley always spoke with great reverence of his enemies. "They were MEN!" he would say with respect. Charley believed strongly that a man was judged not only by his actions, deeds, and friends, but by his enemies as well.

A CHRISTMAS STORY

In the kitchen the cook went to work on the wood stove to prepare a feast of wild turkey and venison. Charley even smiled when the cook went to work, rather than making his usual sour remarks about how the cook had never quite adapted to modern cooking. It was then I notice he had a bottle of "good stuff" hidden in the wood box. For a moment I thought perhaps his merriment could be related to his "tippling" a bit, but I realized it had to be something more than a good bottle because Charley was acting different. He even smiled a little when he talked.

A couple of hours before dinner, Charley disappeared into the back part of his camp. Minutes later he reappeared wearing a suit that had not seen the light since the 1930s. It smelled slightly of moth balls and old pipe tobacco. Even though age had taken its toll on both the man and the suit, had Miss Emma been alive today, she would surely had swooned upon seeing the dashing figure that Charley still was today. It had been Miss Emma, Charley's lady love and wife, who had selected the campsite that Charley called home. On the mantle of the rock fireplace was a faded sepia photograph of a beautiful young woman, a Winchester Model 92 rifle in one hand and a huge whitetail rack in the other. Charley glanced at the photograph as he walked toward us. He stopped momentarily and stared at the photo. A tear came to his eye as he remembered the good times they had shared. He had not worn the suit since her funeral. She had passed away while he was on foray into Mexico. He had never forgiven himself for not being there. If only she could see him now. But she had never been one to dwell on sad moments. The old man straightened, squared his shoulders, and walked to the group.

"Tonight we celebrate! Remember the time I told you about the bandits sharing my fire that cold miserable December night?" I nodded an affirmative. "That night one of them swore if we ever met again, there would be gunplay, and one of us would die. The next day I had him in my sights, then at the last moment just before squeezing the trigger on him, I pulled down and shot his horse out from under him and spared his life." He hesitated momentarily in reflection. "He's alive! I ran into him about a month ago at the Panther Canyon store. We talked for hours, then I invited him to come to dinner. He's coming tonight! My old enemy. Now there was a man!"

That night my old friend said grace . . . "Lord, we thank you for our many blessings. Let us not forget the true meaning of Christmas: to celebrate this time with joy, love, and respect not only for our friends, but for our enemies as well. Amen."

"Amen!"

Dead Sea Snipe

It all started innocently enough. But I should have known something was not quite right when I arrived at high noon at the "Campo del Brasada, Caliente!" hunting camp (which loosely translates to "the hot brush country ain't no place for a gringo to be during the middle of the summer"). The July temperature hovered well over the century mark, yet a crowd comprised primarily of outdoor journalists from across the country had gathered outside. They surrounded what appeared to be a bare spot of red, sandy loam soil. I also noticed a couple had money in their hands, and one held a stopwatch. At first I was reluctant to even get close to the circle, but then I heard someone say, "It's almost there, two minutes and counting!" and curiosity got the better of me. "You're too late for this one!" someone shouted.

I wedged in a little closer to see what all the excitement was about. There on the reddish sandy soil lay a broken eggshell and what appeared to a sunny-side up egg, frying on the bare patch of exposed earth. As I looked on, someone hollered, "It's done, two minutes and forty-three seconds. I win!" That exclamation sparked an argument among the gathered troops as to whether or not the egg was officially fried and done. I felt the best place for me was anywhere else that had shade or was cool. Obviously the South Texas sun was taking its toll on more than the egg.

Upon entering the cool air-conditioned camp, I spotted Hal Swiggett. Besides being a friend, Hal Swiggett has been a hero of mine for years. He is justifiably considered the dean of "gun writers." A native of Kansas but a naturalized Texan, he first served as a newspaper photographer, but he later turned to outdoor journalism and has been writing

PEAR FLAT PHILOSOPHIES

about hunting and guns, especially handguns, since the early 1940s. As an aficionado of handguns, he has no equal! Over the years he has hunted with the likes of Jack O'Connor, Elmer Keith, Bill Jordan, J.D. Jones, and many of the world's foremost hunters. As we visited, Hal asked me to consider hunting with him and a gentleman from Israel that afternoon. Our primary goal would be to find that gentleman a javelina. I felt honored!

Javelina hunting is a pure joy, sometimes, but especially when using an appropriate handgun. Javelina hunting can also be an "iffy" thing. Javelina may be as thick as the proverbial "fleas on a javelina," but finding them can sometimes be difficult, if not downright impossible. Since it was hot enough outside to fry an egg on the bare ground, I doubted seriously whether the little desert pigs would move much before very late in the day. I wanted this to be a successful hunt for everyone, but I wanted my performance to be a triumph—after all, how many times in a lifetime does one get to hunt with one's hero?

In the cool of the camp, Hal and I talked about various handguns and calibers, reminisced of past hunts and mutual friends, and dreamed of future hunts. In short we had a wonderful time. The gentleman from Israel, meanwhile, waited patiently. As the afternoon waned and the hunt for javelina drew near, I warned the hunter from across the seas about javelina, "Probably the worst way to hunt javelina is to hunt javelina. When you do not want them, they pop up out of the ground like ubiquitous jack-in-the-boxes. But go hunt specifically for javelina, and they become scarce as raindrops in a South Texas summer." He smiled and nodded.

One of the better ways to hunt javelina during the summertime is to look for them around water holes. So with about two-hand-heights-below-the-sun left in the sky, we took off to drive the ranch roads and to search for javelina. Each time we approached a stock tank, we would stop and continue on foot. At each stop, we would glass the surrounding areas until our eyes ached. Every water hole was the same: no javelina. As we drove from one supposed "javelina infested" area to another, Hal kept us entertained with talk of new handgun calibers, best loads, and his feats of daring-do on African jungles and plains. His talk of Africa filled us with excitement

DEAD SEA SNIPE

as he described his exploits while stalking wild game with a handgun. His tales were punctuated with pungent remarks about the lack of ability of a certain biologist/scribe/guide's to produce any javelina sightings.

I reminded the gentlemen from across the wide ocean to try to concentrate on anything but hunting javelina . . . rhinos, buffaloes, or mastodons would do. "Keep your mind occupied on anything but the little peccaries," said I. Meanwhile, the sun kept sinking lower and lower—as must have the spirits of our new friend. By this time, he was probably thinking the existence of the javelina or collared peccary was merely a twisted figment of someone's vivid imagination.

When it became so dark that we needed lights to see the ranch road, I looked back at the javelina hunter. He was smiling contentedly. Undoubtedly he was having a good time after all, even though we had not been able to produce a javelina for him. As we headed back to camp, our guest started telling tales of hunting the animals and birds of his homeland. As he spoke, he invited both Hal and me to come hunt with him in Israel, saying that since it was obvious that we truly enjoy hunting the mysterious, elusive phantom of the brush, we must most certainly come to Israel to hunt for an equally elusive quarry, indeed a truly rare bird. The bird he mentioned was one neither Hal nor I, who pride ourselves on our wildlife knowledge, had ever heard of a—perhaps one of you could be of some help. Any chance any of you have heard of the proverbial Dead Sea snipe? I was afraid of that. He did say something about how these snipe were only hunted late at night, in snake-infested swamps, with a gunny sack. . . .

The Young Family

I noticed the young man of seven or eight looking in my direction as I walked into the small restaurant. He was dressed in a Teenage Mutant Ninja Turtle T-shirt, a pair of jeans, and a pair of expensive tennis shoes. He was seated between what were obviously his parents. After sitting down at a table next to them, I listened as the parents spoke in rapt tones of the white-tailed deer they had seen on their trip to some rural community as well as the many songbirds they had heard on their visit to a local state park.

The young man continued to stare in my direction. I tried to pay little mind to his stares while at the same time I felt myself drawn to the conversation of the parents. As a wildlife biologist and writer, I have often found it interesting to listen to the conversations of others. Call it eavesdropping if you wish, but I prefer to call it research. The parents continued speaking of the many facets of the out-of-doors, both plants and animals.

As I had driven into the parking lot, I noticed an expensive car that had several bumper stickers, one of which dealt with saving the whales. Another particularly attractive sticker proclaimed: "Save Wildlife, Shoot a Hunter!" Listening to the couple and their son, I wondered if perhaps the car belonged to them. As I sat there listening, I couldn't help but reflect on their feelings about hunting and wildlife.

Of course I wasn't positive, but it seemed to me that they were probably anti-hunters. The parents appeared to be in their early thirties, their clothing indicated that they were well-to-do, and their conversation showed that they were well-educated. I was nearly certain, after listening to them, that they had grown up in an urban area. I could just imagine how different their beliefs about wildlife, hunting, and guns were from mine. By contrast I had grown up in a rural community where my mother, father, brother, grandfathers, and all our neighbors hunted—giving us, I felt, an understanding of the role of hunting in the natural scheme of things.

The young man continued to stare, and I continued to listen shamelessly. The mother was now talking about how we needed to respect life and how great it was there were still places such as the park they had just visited where people from the cities could see and enjoy wildlife.

In a sideward glance I noticed they were eating salads, even the young man. Vegetarians too, thought I. They surely fit the typical anti-hunting mold.

Glancing across the room the other way, I noticed a pair of rather over-weight women in their mid-forties. What had initially caught my attention was the language they were using. Had I used such words in public or in private while growing up and had my father found out about it, I would not be able to sit for a month. That sort of language I wouldn't even use today, as an adult.

Trying to tune them out, I focused my attention on the conversation next to me. The young man's mother spoke reverently of the land and how all wildlife and man himself depended upon the land and water for life. The young man paid attention and then stated he hoped there would still be wildlife when he grew up and had children of his own. I marveled at the maturity of this child.

Throughout my eavesdropping on the trio's conversation, never had I heard anything about guns and hunting. Although I admit there were times when the loud foul language of the two women in the corner blocked out the conversation next to me.

The young man continued to stare in my direction. As I glanced in his direction I saw him whisper something to his father. With that I turned away to finish my meal before continuing on my journey.

There was a slight tap on my shoulder. Then I heard a very timid, "Mister . . ." I turned to face the young man who had been staring at me. "My Dad and I agree you're the person we have seen in several hunting videos. We watch them all the time! My Dad, Mom, and I would like for you to join us at our table. Would you please. . . .?"

Now, how could I refuse a request like that?

As I got up to move to their table, I watched the two foul-mouthed women from the corner table get up and walk out to their expensive gas-guzzling car with the anti-hunter bumper stickers. My grandpa was right about many things, but never more so than when he told me: "Never judge a book by its cover!"

The Bet

I first met the Cap'n during my serious traveling days. At the time I was a biologist traveling throughout the state of Texas, working somewhat as a troubleshooter on various projects and doing research concerning wildlife diseases and white-tailed deer nutrition. Other than being away from my bride and our then young daughters, it was a good and interesting time. Beyond getting to see new country, it gave me the opportunity to meet quite a few "characters." It was on one of those sojourns into the western hills of the Big Bend area that I ran into the Cap'n. After having collected some sick deer just west of the Louisiana-Texas border, I had driven most of the day and the night before to reach the little Trans-Pecos town. Although sleep beckoned, I knew there was just enough time for a cup of coffee and breakfast before having to meet a rancher about what might be causing the death of several mule deer on his ranch.

Seated at a table was a man who looked to be in his late sixties or early seventies. He wore a tall-crowned hat, red bandanna, starched white shirt, jeans, and tall-heeled riding boots; he had stuffed his pants in his boot tops. His hands were steady, but his face looked like a topographic map of steep rough country. His gray handlebar moustache drooped a bit, hiding his ready smile. From under the brim of his hat, his steel-gray eyes watched my every movement as I walked in.

Since it was still a solid two hours before daylight, I was only able to manage a less-than-my-usual-chirpy "Howdy!" as I walked by. Seeing him sitting there he reminded me of my paternal grandfather, who had dressed in a similar fashion. The old man nodded, acknowledging my presence.

PEAR FLAT PHILOSOPHIES

"Where ya headed this morning Colorado (which he pronounced cahlah-rou, apparently because of my red hair and moustache)? Kinda early for a youngster like you to be up, ain't it? Or are you just a-coming in?"

I responded by telling my purpose for being in the area and what we hoped to accomplish while there. He graciously gave me directions to the ranch where they had been losing the mule deer. He was also quick to point out what he thought might know the cause for losing deer on the ranch in question.

"Those deer are dying of a pretty common disease, 'specially on that place and several others around here. Ain't nothing more but hollow belly. Damn ol' domestic sheep eat everything that grows on that place. If it looks like the green is catching up a bit, damn fool goes out and buys more sheep. Ain't ever seen the likes of someone so 'fraid that one leaf grown won't be et! Go on out there and see for yourself. If I'm right, stop by the ranch this evening and I'll show you what this country ought to look like." With that he handed me a map drawn on the back of a napkin that showed me how to get to his ranch. "By the way, my friends call me Cap'n!" said he, as he extended his right hand when I got up to leave. Several hours and many bouncing, dusty, rocky roads later, I realized the elderly gentleman I had met before daylight was right. For the most part the deer were simply starving to death.

Late that same evening I drove to the old rancher's headquarters. When I arrived, he was sitting out in front of an attractive rock house watching the sun go down from his rocking chair. No sooner had I stopped the truck than he greeted me with, "Well, Colorado what'd you find?" Before I could answer, he hollered, "Consuela, bring my new-found friend here a couple of jiggers of whiskey . . . and you might just as well bring us the bottle while you're at it!" Then staring hard in my direction, he said, "Well . . . whadya find?"

"We spent the better part of the day looking at rocks and bare dirt. Little wonder why those deer were dying," said I as I sipped the Cap'n's wondrous golden elixir and watched the old man's contented rocking.

"What'd you tell them the problem was?" queried the Cap'n.

"I told him he had too much shade," said I as I took another sip.

[130]

THE BET

"Shade?" laughed the old man, not missing a beat.

"Yes, sir. I told him he had so many sheep in that country they were blocking out the sunshine—it was no wonder there was nothing growing and the deer were dying."

At my reasoned appraisal of the rancher's plight, the Cap'n laughed so hard he nearly fell out of his rocker. It was from this auspicious beginning that our predestined relationship began. In subsequent visits to the area I always made it a point to stop in to see him, normally with a bottle of good Irish whiskey in hand. We would then visit throughout the night—not breaking off until Consuela would get up with the rising sun and start the coffee. Mostly I would listen to Cap'n telling tales of his hunting trips for grizzly bear and sheep in the late 1940s, his trips to Africa even earlier, and his stories of what the surrounding country was like when desert bighorn sheep still roamed the area.

A year had passed since our last palaver before I again saw the Cap'n—but this time he was a considerable number of miles down the Rio Grande, near the sleepy little village of Quemada, just down from Eagle Pass. After greeting one another, I asked him why he was so far from home.

"Going on my annual dove hunt in Mexico. Park your rig and go with me—won't be gone long, probably be back this afternoon."

In spite of having things to do and places to go I decided to switch priorities. A couple hours later we were approaching a grain field south of the Rio Grande. The hunt had been set up by a local Mexican government official for an old friend and several young businessmen, from north of the Rio Bravo. There were already several hunters near our field as we walked up. Most were dressed as if they had just stepped out of a international dove hunter's style show. The shotguns they carried were Parkers and finely inlaid European doubles, whose maker's names I have still not learned how to pronounce.

The Cap'n walked up carrying his shiny (as in down to raw metal, with the blueing worn off) Winchester Model 12 and wearing a sweat-stained felt, a long-sleeved white shirt, faded red neckerchief, and equally faded jeans. The younger men were all decked out in fancy hunting duds—looking like models for a magazine ad or caricatures of what they supposed hunters to look like. As soon as we walked up, this group of dandies started making fun of the Cap'n's old pump shotgun and how the old man was dressed. They were righteous in their belief that "everyone" had to wear camouflage, and not a white shirt, when hunting doves. They were merciless about the shiny, timeworn shotgun—ibelieving that the gun would spook every dove in the field. The old man simply smiled at their taunts.

Perhaps it was the tequila and hot sun that caused them to talk as they did. The Cap'n, however, took little notice of their talk. He smiled as the younger men bragged about the prices they had paid for their fancy firearms of steel and wood, and he simply listened and sized up each of them as they talked of all the fancy hunting lodges where they had shot . . . from the quail plantations of Georgia to driven partridge in Spain

I stood off to the side watching the Cap'n. With the gaze of a gunfighter, he sized up each of the shooters as he watched them shoot. The Cap'n just stood there, watching. Finally one of the set shouted at the Cap'n:

"What's a matter old man, we too quick for you? Or don't you know how to shoot that piece of junk you carrying?"

"Young man, you're pretty free with your mouth; you got any money to back up your words?" shot back the old man. By then it was obvious that

THE BET

the hot sun, ego, bravado, and tequila were clouding the younger man's brain.

"Five hundred says you can't hit ten birds in a row!" spoke one from under his Panama-style hat. Two others hurriedly hollered, "I'll take some of the action!"

The Cap'n looked over my way, winked, and then turned to those who had finally put their money where their mouths were. "Tell ya'll what, make it an even thousand per person for the next twenty birds in a row, and you got yourself a bet!"

PEAR FLAT PHILOSOPHIES

"Easy money, boys!" bragged the original blowhard.

Up until the bet the birds had been coming over rather sporadically. But almost as if on cue, the evening flights to the grain fields started trickling by.

"I'll take the one on the far right, then the next one to it, and finish with the one on the far left," said the Cap'n as he brought the old Model 12 to his shoulder. Three shots blasted and three whitewings were ready for the bird-boys to go pick up. In rapid order seventeen more shots put seventeen more birds on the ground. The Cap'n then turned to the previously boisterous trio and said, "Pay up!"

Reluctantly they dug into their pockets and produced neatly folded one hundred dollar bills, twenty-nine of them plus four twenties, leaving them scarcely enough pocket change to pay the toll to get them back across the border.

"Gentlemen," said he with a tip of his hat. "It's been a pleasure!"

Then turning to me he said, "Colorado looks like we got us enough money for supper and a bottle of good stuff. You might as well just plan on spending the night with me in Del Rio. I'll call your bride and tell her I kidnapped you!"

As we walked away I could hear the betters talking to our host, "Who the hell was that old bastard anyway?"

"Oh compadre, ju chould af known more better! De Cap'n he has schot with me many, many times. In twenty-five jears of chuting palomas, he hass nevver missed a schot. De Cap'n hee's de onliest hombre in history to be de internatchonal live pigeon chuter cinco times, si five times. *Hee's muy bueno cazadoro, no?*"

As the Cap'n walked away carrying his time-polished Model 12 tucked neatly under his arm, he turned to me and repeated an ancient Persian proverb taught to him by his father: "If he plays, being young and skillful, for shekels of silver or gold, take his money, my son, and praise Allah! The lamb was ordained to be sold." The bulge in the old man's pocket would certainly keep him in Irish whisky and vittles for quite some time to come!

A Letter to Texas

During a happily misspent lifetime of frequenting hunting camps, presiding and indulging in campfire "meetings," and having kicked around a bit throughout North America, I have run into my share of characters. Some were unforgettable, some I could not wait to forget, and some thankfully turned out to be true friends whose friendships I highly value. All too often great distances separate, and it is only on rare occasions that there is an opportunity to sit down and visit for a while. It is unfortunate, but some of those friendships have drifted by the wayside, and we seldom even write anymore. Thankfully a few persist.

One of the characters it has been my pleasure to call a friend resides near the north Texas town of Clifton—that is, when he is not trailing hounds somewhere in North America or for that matter looking at fine English foxhounds and coursing the moors across the Atlantic. Among other things he is a retired wildlife biologist. Quite a few years ago when most of us biologists had not even heard the term, "non-game species," my friend was the spokesman for the fox, coyote, bobcat, and raccoon—the sort of animal that brings great pleasure to those who enjoy listening to a good pack of trailing or treeing hounds.

My friend, Joe Stevens, is also somewhat of a "country preacher," spreading the message of the Gospel wherever he travels. When Joe and I were on the road together, years ago, many were the nights we spent discussing religion. Joe had a knack of helping people understand things more clearly than anyone I have ever known. Having grown up on a ranch out in the country and having served some time in hell during the Second World War, Joe had a way of relating God's plans for all in everyday ranch terms.

PEAR FLAT PHILOSOPHIES

It was after Joe retired that we began exchanging letters. He would write about how his Walker hounds were progressing, which incidentally are some of the best in all of North America, and in turn I would write of my adventures in chasing big racked white-tailed bucks through the prickly pear flats. In time we simply drifted apart and quit writing, except for a rare card near Christmas. Not very long ago, however, I received a short note from Joe, actually written to and delivered by a mutual friend. With this friend's permission, I would like to quote from the letter:

"Thanks for contacting Larry and for sending me his article about the big buck. I know he likes to chase deer, but he also likes to hunt with hounds, so I am hoping that he will come hunt with me later this year when the rattlesnakes are denned up. I'd like to share a bear story with him, which I'm sure he'll enjoy.

While in Alaska this summer we saw eight wild grizzlies. They were quite some distance away and I really wanted to observe them up close; however, the park ranger would not let me get closer, nor would he allow me to take a gun into Denali National Park. After leaving the park but still wanting to get a closer look at a wild grizzly, I found an old "nester" who lived just outside the park. After talking to him for a while, he agreed to let me go down the river by his place to study the bears. He suggested I borrow a gun from him, in case I got into trouble, which I did. As we talked, he told me about trying to raise cattle in that part of the country. He said he had several cows and bulls shipped in from down south to try to start a little herd of cattle, but the grizzlies had taken to beef and had killed all but one ornery old bull. And he was meaner than a grizzly, so I should watch out for him when I headed down to the river.

Well, I was easing down a trail near the river thinking about ol' Ephram when all of a sudden, lo and behold, a big blond grizzly appeared in the middle of my trail, coming from the bank of the river, heading my way. He shook himself, woofed, then popped his teeth, and came down the trail straight in my direction! My head said, "DON'T PANIC," but my legs said, "RUN!" As I turned around to retreat, would you believe, standing not six feet away and staring directly at me was the

A LETTER TO TEXAS

bull, madly pawing dirt!! For sure I had to make a fast decision—what would you have done? So I took quick and careful aim and shot the ol' grizzly. Figured I could wait until I got back to Texas to `Shoot the Bull!!' Best of everything!"

Your friend,

Joe

LESOB

When the telephone rang, I was reluctant to answer, but then I got to thinking . . . it might really be something important! Who knows? It could be someone calling to invite me on an all-expense paid hunt for Canadian whitetails, or the tax man might be calling to tell me I had been granted a tax-free status, or possibly a local friend was calling to invite me for coffee at the local caffeine cantina. Still unsure as to whether the advantages outweighed the disadvantages, I let the pleading phone erupt with one more shrill call before I gave in. It was someone trying to sell me a magazine subscription to a publication that opposed the right to bear arms and to hunt. Boy did she ever get the wrong number!

It did, however, bring to mind some incidents that happened a few years ago, and it reminded me that sometimes pure anticipation is the only reward received in an endeavor. In other words, suppose you have just spotted the lady of your dreams—a vision of loveliness with the face of an angel and the body of a goddess? You finally build up enough courage to approach her. She turns to greet you and acknowledges your presence with a shy smile. You stammer as you introduce yourself—"not a good beginning" you chide yourself silently. But then your vision replies—with a voice that sounds like someone scratching a chalkboard or with a mouthful of black teeth—and your vision evaporates before your very eyes. Well, sometimes life is like that.

As a youngster I grew up around horses. My father and grandfather, who shared the joint philosophy that it was next to sinful to walk anywhere, taught me to ride and to respect horses from an early age. It was during those early, formative years that I developed a great liking for long-eared mules. I can still remember how I longed to own a good riding mule and a string of pack mules. Unfortunately, back then my only acquaintance with a mule was staring at the backside of my granddad's old plow mule as my dad unsuccessfully tried to teach me how to plow a straight row in our family's garden. It soon became obvious that plowing with a mule was a talent I lacked: My rows were about as straight as the strands of

cooked spaghetti. I knew from those early frustrating attempts at plowing that I was not cut out to be a farmer, but I continued dreaming of owning a good riding mule. I'm sure that this desire was a result of overdosing on hunting magazines and daydreaming of pack-string hunting trips to the mountains.

During the ensuing years I had, on numerous occasions, ridden mules in the hills and even occasionally when working cattle. But my first real chance at owning my own mules came after I moved to the West Texas town of Abilene. For years several friends and I had been hunting mule deer and elk in Colorado and New Mexico, and each year we would use local rented horses and mules to pack into the back country. One day we started "figuring" the cost of renting horses and mules each year for our outings, and we decided that we could just as easily and more economically own our own string of mules. The cost split between those who used the mules would make it easily affordable and lessen the burden for all. With that, we established a "mule fund" and began the arduous task and chore of locating good riding and packing mules. One in our midst, with time on his hands and a proclaimed experienced "mule pilot" was designated the chief mule procurer.

Within less than a month, we had a string of mules, the lucky number totaled thirteen to be exact. I use the term "string" (which might denote somewhat equally sized beasts of burden) loosely, because our mules ranged in height from what appeared to be about eight hands to well over twenty hands. If that sounds like they ranged in size from about mid-thigh to well over six feet tall at the withers, you have got the correct picture. But then again, maybe the selection simply reflected the various sizes of the partners involved. The head mule procurer proclaimed he had been told all the mules in our string were broken to ride and/or pack. After dealing with these mangy monsters for a few days, I suspect the mule seller would also have been just as truthful if he had sworn all these mules could fly as well.

We made arrangements to pasture the mules about twenty-five miles from town on a mutual friend's ranch. (What he failed to tell us was that he was planning on using the mules for bucking practice to further his rodeo career when we were not around.) Once we had the mules properly pastured, we started on the long arduous task of working with the stock to get them into riding and packing shape before the beginning of the fast-approaching hunting season. It did not take Chuck Dalchau (who had done a little bit of rodeoing in his younger days) and me long to determine that out of the thirteen mules we had only a couple that had ever had a saddle on its back. We figured, if we were lucky, one just might have been packed in the past. We had our work cut out for us.

Out of the string, I selected two mules, both about 750 pounds in weight, with good confirmation and an intelligent look in their eyes. One was a beautiful blue roan. The other a yellow dun with a dark brown stripe right down the middle of his back and brown tiger stripes on his lower legs. Naturally the roan became "Ol' Blue." The dun, well . . . he eventually earned his name.

Ol' Blue had a nice even temperament and, with very little work, reined like a good cowhorse and was a pleasure to ride. His gait was long and smooth. The dun was somewhat of a free spirit. The first time I put a rope around his neck, he bared his teeth and did his darnedest to bite me. He pitched and bucked as soon as I put on a saddle blanket and saddle. With the help of a friend, I was finally able to cinch him up a bit. But he continued pitching and bucking until the only man-made substance remaining on his body was the rope. After three such incidents, I seriously considered changing the bowline knot to a hangman's noose.

After several days of biting my tongue and using some truly selective vocabulary to describe the dun and his entire family ancestry, I was finally able to saddle him and put fore and aft breechings on him so he would not be able to rid himself of the saddle. Then came the time to ride him. Pulling my hat down on my ears, I crawled aboard as two friends held him, one with his mouth full of mule ear. No sooner was I firmly planted in the saddle than they released him. Immediately the dun started to pitch, buck, fishtail, bite, and snort. I held tight and spurred whenever the opportunity arose. After what seemed an eternity of his bucking, I felt the tail-breeching break. Next thing I knew, even though still in the saddle, I was riding his neck just behind those long ears. With his next move the saddle with me still intact pitched over his ears and onto the hard, dusty ground.

This same sort of bucking went on every time I was able to get a saddle on his back. I most certainly did not relish the thought of riding the dun over some narrow mountainous trails in the high country. Try as I might, he never did settle down to be a riding mule. If he could not buck you off, he would throw himself over backward and then roll on the saddle. This pack mule was a real gem.

I guess there was one good thing that came out of all that "mule exercising." The dun finally earned himself a name, LESOB. The LE stands for Long Eared, and I'll let you guess what the rest stands for! As I said in the beginning of this epistle, sometimes you think you have finally found the love of your life only to find the anticipation is just about as good as it's going to get . . . and the reality sometimes "purty" ain't near what it's made out to be!

Old Clothes

"What in the world is this pile of rags doing in the house?" asked my wife as she passed through the family room. Then before I could answer, she chortled: "Hallelujah! You're finally getting rid of the stuff that's been cluttering up our clothes closet for the last twenty-five years. I knew one of these days you would come to your senses and get rid of that stuff. Why, most of those . . . ah, those hunting clothes, as you call them wouldn't even make decent rags. Although it looks as if there might be one or two that might not get thrown away by the Goodwill people. Tell you what, let's make three piles. One for the Goodwill box, one to use for dust rags, and one for the garbage men. And by the looks of what I can see, the garbage men are going to get the bulk of that pile!" By the look in the biscuit maker's eye, she was dead serious.

"Er . . . ah . . . well . . . " was all I could stutter. "That's not exactly what I had in mind. You know hunting season starts in a few days and I . . . ah, well . . . I was just getting together a few things and hoping you might wash them for me." With perspiration dripping, I manfully managed to mutter: "I was just sorting through them to be sure I didn't leave anything in the pockets." Just at that moment I reached my favorite camo jacket and found a chocolate candy bar I thought I had lost two years ago while hunting elk in the high country. In the other pocket was a dried apple and two spent .280 Remington cases.

"Wash these clothes? Why I doubt they would survive a good washing. That shirt (pointing at my favorite, "lucky" plaid) would go to pieces and clog the machine and drain. No, I think the best thing we could do is for you to throw them all away. Besides most of what you have there is tattered, worn, and full of holes—shirts as well as pants. I know we're poor, but that's no excuse for you to be seen in public with holey shirts and pants."

"But dear you don't understand! I like wearing those holey shirts and pants. They're finally getting comfortable. You cannot imagine all I have endured to get those clothes to the comfortable stage. Why it's taken me years of crawling through catclaw and wait-a-minute brush to get them where they are today. Actually they are like fine pieces of art and wine that increase in value with time, same as old friends. They also serve as a scrapbook of memories."

Picking up the green plaid I bravely continued, "See this rip right here (pointing to a long tattered tear on the right upper sleeve). This happened several years ago when Porter and I were hunting together just south of Hebbronville in what used to be called the Wild Horse Desert. We jumped a big twelve-point buck just as the sun went down. I took off after him at a run, hoping to get a shot as he reappeared on the other side of the thicket—problem was I didn't know about or see the rusty barbed-wire fence, hidden there in the thicket."

I glanced at my wife and noticed the knuckles of her closed fists planted firmly against her hips were starting to regain some of the natural color as she started to relax just a bit.

Thinking my strategy was working, I continued, "And this small rip (only an eight-inch tattered gash) on the left elbow happened the year before we were married: Glenn and I were stalking a pretty fair buck, but to get closer I had to elbow crawl nearly 300 yards over dry sandstone. I never would have torn the sleeve if I hadn't been in a hurry, but I had a date with you later that evening and wanted to be there on time! Then this one over here. . . ." At that point I could see she was starting to come over to my side of thinking, when she interrupted me with a heavy sigh.

"OK, you win. Start putting them in the washing machine. But you better really be careful to be sure there is nothing strange in those pockets. I'm warning you, if you left a container of skunk scent in one of those pockets, I'm outa here! Forever!!!" said she of the fairer sex, shaking her right index finger right under my nose. At that point she and I started laughing, both obviously recalling a friend of our's whose wife had washed a hunting coat that contained a full bottle of skunk scent. That load of clothes never again quite smelled like daisies in the springtime, and, as I remember it now, the couple divorced before the beginning of the next hunting season.

"I've warned you!" said the love of my life as she stalked out of the room.

Men, have you ever noticed how most wives simply have no real appreciation for hunting season's comfortable clothes or hats? Each year my wife and I go through the same ritual. To me, my hunting clothes truly are like old friends, and a friendship they have earned. The same is true of old felt hats. To my wife they are a source of embarrassment.

Nearly all my life I have worn western felt hats. Although I admit having slipped a bit during the urban cowboy movie craze, several years ago when I quit wearing a hat for about two years! But I certainly did not get rid of my old friends. Currently my "old" hat looks just like an old hat should. It proudly shows its many years of use and abuse, from the sweat-stained brim to its tattered crown. That old hat has been with me from thin to thick and back to thin again. It's shown up in Canada and in Mexico, and even made a trip to France with me a few years ago. It's even survived a few gunfights!

My "new" old hat also wears its past proudly. But I am afraid the time I lost it for a couple of weeks when it blew off my head and out the open cockpit of a helicopter set it on some hard times. By the time I recovered it, my hat had unceremoniously become home for a pair of kangaroo rats. However, all in all it survived the ordeal fairly well. It too has served me well through desert dust storms and Rocky Mountain blizzards.

I strongly believe hunting season is a time for old friends to get together, and certainly my old hunting clothes rank in the highest circle. Hunting without them would be almost as bad as never being able to again hunt wily old gnarled antlered white-tailed bucks!

Now if I can just come up with a good way to infiltrate some of my other old friends that I have hidden in several duffel bags in my office into our bedroom closet. . . . Guess I could always say they belonged to you, and I was just taking care of them for you . . . but then again, my wife is probably

wise to my ploys by now because she and I have already gone
through all that with hounds and dogs. . . . Never owned
one myself, you understand, but have taken care of the mailman's
bear dogs, our insurance salesman's hog dogs, my brother and
Dad's coon hounds, the next door neighbor's pointers, my
cousin's fox hounds, the rabbit dogs that "belonged" to the kid
down the street. . . .

Forks of the Creek

"That damn ol' coon has been taking those hounds through some of the thickest country we got. Several years ago some cedar-whackers moved in and cut most of the cedar. What grew up in its place was nothing but green briars and youpon so thick a skinny snake can hardly get through. There's ol' Rip. Sounds like they are gaining on him. Must have gotten him back in some of the more open country. Listen!" demanded my dad.

Off in the distance, barely within hearing was a pack of seven hounds trailing a raccoon. "They're heading the other direction. Let's go!" With that we took off at a trot, me having to take four steps to every one of my father's.

Just as I was about to make my way through a thicket, a previously held limb, at the hand of one of my dad's hunting partners, was released. It struck swiftly and solidly across my face, sending my eyeglasses flying into the darkness. With blurred vision, I could barely make out the rapidly disappearing light of the man in front. The night was as black as liquid ink. The only stars I saw were those exploding in my head. Dropping to my hands and knees, the search for the glasses began. The night amplified every sound from the barking of the hounds now just barely audible to the distant "whooing" of an owl. I groped around in the darkness complaining about the limb, my eyeglasses, the lack of a carbide lantern or flashlight, and just about anything else that came to mind!

I knew my dad would follow the hounds; chances were he was trotting along behind them by now. All evening I had felt like the only reason he had not kept up with the hounds all along was because I was slowing him down. Now I had lost my eyeglasses and my face hurt—it was too much! Irritation, anger, and even despair welled up within. I knew six-year old cowboys were not supposed to shed tears, but I was just about to that point when I heard a rustling noise.

The sounds of footsteps were easily discernible on the late winter, leaf-strewn ground. For a moment I imagined all sorts of evil, which might be coming to prey on my almost helpless situation. What if it were a stranger, possibly an outlaw hiding from the law—or a bear, even though there had not been a bear seen in these parts in over eighty years? What if it was the neighbor's bull? I was in for it if it was the neighbor's bull—the last time I had come through this field in the daylight heading to one of my favorite fishing holes, the old bull had chased me over a good part of the pasture. I had finally eluded him by crawling up a tree. "Oh, please don't let it be the bull!" I murmured.

The footsteps came closer. I stopped, still on all fours, and remained as quiet as possible. The only sounds I could hear were the pounding of my heart in my ears and . . . whatever was coming increasingly nearer. When you are six years old . . . well, your imagination can run rampant. Even though I was wise to the woods and its creatures, I was still on all fours in an inky-black night, I had no glasses or flashlight, and something was coming my way. I had the possible danger narrowed down to the neighbor's bull, a homicidal maniac just escaped from an insane asylum, a rogue grizzly bear with a sweet tooth for young cowboys, a werewolf that did not like full-moon nights, and . . . Just then the sound charged in my direction. Before I could even begin to react, a hot, wet tongue licked its way across my face.

"EEEEEEOOOOOOOOOOOOOOOOOOOOWWWWWWWWWWWWW!" screamed the terrified six-year old cowboy! Forgetting about lost glasses, being Roy Rogers brave, or anything else short of simple survival, I jumped up and started running mostly in the same place but gaining just enough forward movement to run nose first into a tree. Dazed, I fell over backward knowing full well I was dead meat. Almost immediately I felt a warm liquid spurt from my "squished" nose. The sound of whatever had attacked me was right at my side. Before I could move, the savage creature straddled me with its four legs and began licking and nudging my face. I reached up to grab the ferocious beast by the neck to fend myself from his attempts to eat me alive.

FORKS OF THE CREEK

But then I felt something familiar. It was a dog collar! The collar that belonged to "Ol' Blue," my Dad's bluetick hound. He and I had sort of grown up together. Realizing it was Blue, I reached up and gave him a hug. I was thankful to be alive, yet feeling a bit stupid about my actions and my bloody nose. As I dropped my arms back to the ground, my right hand touched an object that felt like it did not belong with the sticks and leaves littering the ground . . . ah, life is good—I had found my glasses!

Hurriedly I put the glasses on, reached into my hip pocket for my red bandanna (all cowboys carry big, red bandannas) for just such emergencies. I wiped the blood from my face and then tied the bandanna to Blue's collar. Together we made our way through the darkness toward the sounds of the hounds that had treed the raccoon. As Blue and I approached the tree, my dad shined the light our way.

"They got him!" he shouted, and then he asked, "You OK?"

"Yes sir, Blue and I are fine. Boy he's a big one!" said I pointing to the old ringtailed bandit sitting in the safety of the upper limbs of the tree.

Later that night as we drove the old pickup back home, I said: "Daddy I think I've come to that fork in the creek you've been telling me about. . . ." I am sure he wondered how a six-year old could have come "to the fork of the creek," but he patiently listened to my plans for the future.

It was not until many years later that my dad and I spoke of that long-ago night. This time we were with hounds for black bear high in the mountains of New Mexico. As we stared into the flames fueled by an alligator juniper stump my father spoke, "Remember that time when we treed that old hard-running 'coon behind the house? You were six. We left you behind after you lost your glasses. Then you bumped into that tree and bloodied your nose. That old blue dog was something special, wasn't he?"

I must have swallowed a bit hard. Until that moment I had never told anyone about what had happened, nor was I even aware anyone knew of the incident. That old blue dog might have been something special, but so was the man who had watched over his freckle-faced son and provided guidance . . . even when things seemed the darkest.

[151]

The Old Hunter

The old man wanted to go hunting again. His rifle had been oiled to the point of gleaming. His hunting knife honed to an edge even the most critical surgeon would have appreciated. His bags had been packed for months. Each day he checked and double checked the contents to be sure he would have all the needed essentials, not only cartridges, clothes, gear, but a packet of his secret chili fixings as well.

As the cool breezes of fall started blowing southward, he had begun to feel better. Gone were his normal aches and pains. Sleep came readily at the end of each day, and each morning arrived with a promise. Afternoon naps were filled with dreams of hunting seasons past. Old friends and hunting partners were fondly recalled, even though some had passed on to their rewards.

One afternoon he dreamed of hunting in the rugged, moon-like mountains of Texas's Trans-Pecos region, just south of the sleepy village of Marfa. It was during the early 1950s, a time he happily remembered when few ventured westward to hunt the desert, mule-eared blacktail. With donkeys and mules they had packed wall tents, a sheepherder stove and sufficient "vittles" into the back country for a two-week stay in the desert mountains.

The area was rugged and remote, and the rancher who had provided the stock had told them that no one had hunted the area, save possibly bandits and Indians of long ago. It had taken two mule-stubborn days to pack into the chosen canyon. The only signs of civilization they had found on the trek were a few stone arrowheads and pottery chards. Mule deer sign was abundant. On the pack trip they had occasionally spooked not only mule deer, but the diminutive fantail whitetail as well.

PEAR FLAT PHILOSOPHIES

Camp was set up in an area near a *tenajo*, as the Mexicans called pools of water created by a spring.

He awoke with the acrid smell of greasewood smoke still fresh in his nostrils. For a moment he didn't know where he was—he could hardly believe he had been dreaming. But then he looked up from his easy chair, and there on the wall were the mounts of mule deer and fantail he had taken so long ago.

As he gazed at them, he again relived the hunt. He chuckled to himself as he remembered the day ol' Slim, his hunting partner, unknowingly had sat down on a clump of prickly pear as he prepared to get off a shot at a monstrous mule deer. Most of the rest of the trip Slim ate standing up and slept on his stomach.

When the ride to the hunting camp arrived, he was ready to go. "Think I'll take another eight-point this year?" asked a young blonde-haired granddaughter of her granddad as they drove past the city limits sign. The old man nodded an affirmative, vividly recalling the day, seemingly now only a few days ago, when his own daughter had spent time with him in hunting camp.

THE OLD HUNTER

The old man listened to the conversation of his two granddaughters as they recalled past hunts with their father. The grandfather had committed to memory their stories and quickly reminded them about details he recalled that they might have otherwise forgotten.

PEAR FLAT PHILOSOPHIES

He had memorized their deer hunting stories to the exact details including the pauses in the previous tellings. When the conversation slowed, he asked them how they had felt immediately after taking their bucks. He reminded them one must always be respectful of the animals they hunted and took. He also reminded them hunting was a privilege, one which must be cherished and protected. As the miles stacked up he recalled some of his past hunting seasons. He remembered the days when white-tailed deer were scarce, not nearly as plentiful as they were today.

One particular buck stood out in his memory, which he had hunted for a couple of years. Numerous hunters had seen it and some had even taken shots at the buck, but never had the deer been brought down. The buck soon came to be known as the "phantom." After many hours of "studying" the situation, he decided to hunt a small thicket fairly close to town, an area a bit out of the "phantom's" normal area. No sooner had he slipped into the downwind side of the thicket than he saw the deer. A snap shot fell the monster. To attest to the buck's past good luck, there embedded in an antler was a "00" buckshot. Thereafter the buck held a place of honor in his home.

To the old man it really made little difference whether or not he actually got to hunt during the upcoming season. Being in hunting camp was the important thing, to spend time with his family, smell the aroma of strong hunting-camp coffee, of eggs and bacon frying in a black, cast-iron skillet. The importance lay in being there, sitting around the crackling cedar fire and gazing into the coals of mesquite long into the night. To recall past experiences to an audience who was genuinely interested in hunting-camp tales and to argue with old friends about the best deer calibers and rifle, these were reasons enough to be in hunting camp and to look toward the fall each year with great anticipation. These were the memories that lasted long after the glow of the present campfire had dimmed.

Graves

The north wind blew with such force I suspected I could have hurled myself off the nearby bluff overlooking a nameless Wyoming creek, and it would have blown me backward beyond from where I had initiated the jump. Thankfully I had the good sense not to try. The winds had blown every day since my arrival, and I guess it had started getting to me.

Sitting in the pickup I got tickled watching a pair of golden eagles riding the currents. When they attempted to fly into the wind, they hung there without any forward movement, yet, when they decided to fly with the wind, it took all the aeronautical skills they could muster to remain aloft. Watching them, I wished I had the ability to simply fly over rolling sagebrush hills and cottonwood-studded creek bottoms to locate the white-tailed deer we anxiously hunted.

For the past few days Richard Edwards and I had been doing our best to locate a decent whitetail in the windy, wide-open plains of eastern Wyoming. The Cowboy State's special late white-tailed deer season had lured me northward out of my home in the mesquite and prickly pear country of the Southwest.

In the Texas panhandle, there is a saying that the only thing that separates the Panhandle from the North Pole is a rusty barbed-wire fence. The winds of December blow cold in the north country, and in northeastern Wyoming it seemed the rusted barbed-wire fence must have been considerably farther south. Intermittently the gray skies spit out a bit of snow. With any luck, the ground would be blanketed by morning, revealing ideal tracking snow. I was daydreaming of great northern bucks when Richard spoke.

"The Oregon Trail ran right near here. Back when I was a kid growing up in these parts I used to fish this stretch of creek. Just around the bend is where the travelers crossed the stream in their ox-drawn Conestoga wagons. It must have been a sight to behold, a line of wagons heading for the promised land. Imagine the things they saw: great herds of buffalo, elk, and pronghorn antelope—and the hardships they endured. The thought of wintering in this country in a wagon or dugout isn't too appetizing. 'Course they probably didn't know they were not well off or that times were really hard."

He hesitated and then asked, "You in for a little walk? I can drop you off here and then pick you up about a mile or so from here, just up the creek. If you'll stay on the edge of the ridge overlooking the bottom, you'll likely see some whitetails, maybe even a mulie or two. Earlier in the year I saw some really good bucks in this area, including one big, heavy-horned deer. He's just eight points, but he's a dandy!"

I have long prided myself about hunting in horrible weather, quite often when most other hunters are in camp. I enjoy the solitude of such times. Thus I jumped at the opportunity.

GRAVES

With scarcely a "See you later," I took off slowly walking along the edge of the creek, excuse me "crik." The wind continued to blow at gale force causing the bits of frozen rain and snow to sting when they struck my exposed skin. But between concentrating on looking for game and enjoying the moment, I scarcely noticed the weather.

It was about thirty minutes after leaving Richard that I walked on the backside of a rise in the creek bank and walked up on a gravesite. The headstone was somewhat askew and the iron picket fence could have used some straightening. At first I was fascinated by the sight, but then as I approached, I did so with a certain amount of trepidation. In the eerie gray light of the wintry late afternoon, I could scarcely make out the scratching on the sandstone headstone.

Best as I could discern without getting too close, the inscription on the stone read "Betsy, Loving Daughter Age 12, Killed by Indians, December, 1878." For a moment I was stabbed by the same grief the young girl's family must have felt. My younger daughter's name is Elizabeth, and she too would be twelve in only a few days. Suddenly I felt chilled by more than the icy north winds. Taken by the moment, I murmured a small prayer and then stood in silence before turning and making my way to the western slope of the small hill overlooking the stream, now iced over except for a mere trickle.

As I started toward a better vantage point of the bottom, I glanced at a badger hole dug into the western slope of the creek bank. There protruding from the upper edge of the diggings was the remains of a human skull and several arrow and lance points made of flint that had been buried with the body. The eerie feeling returned as I stared at what seemed to be the remains of an ancient Indian warrior placed so he could forever see the westward setting sun.

I wondered if the parents of the young girl who had been killed in an Indian attack knew they had buried their daughter within mere feet of where an Indian warrior was buried. Or would they have cared? Then I wondered if it would matter. Momentarily all thoughts of white-tailed deer were forgotten. In the distance I thought I heard the soft giggle of a young girl. Then the piercing sound of an ancient high pitched war cry intermingled with the more girlish giggling. The ghostly sounds seemed in harmony. I smiled, wiped the wind-caused tear from my eye, turned toward the north, and walked on.

Whitetail Techniques With a Few Grains of Salt!

Perspiration dripped onto my glasses as I meshed the tines of my rattling horns. Hunting season had begun at daylight, ushered in by a coyote serenade and temperatures in the low 80s. According to all the authorities, it was much too early in November to rattle up bucks in South Texas. Supposedly it was also much too hot: By shortly after sunrise, the temperature hovered just below the century mark. Undaunted, I continued "tickling" my rattling horns—in this case, large mule-deer sheds.

Almost immediately a massive-antlered buck charged out of a nearby thicket. By the time I had laid down the rattling horns and picked up my old Remington, the buck had come within three yards of my position, almost close enough to touch with my rifle barrel. Not finding his imagined fight, he started circling my position, allowing me the opportunity to shoulder the .280 and simply point the rifle in his direction and fire, much like shooting a shotgun. Immediately the buck went down. By the time I finished the field-dressing chores and dragged him to my Jeep Cherokee, I was sopping wet with perspiration.

By all rights I should never have rattled up that buck, those numerous years ago. Everyone "knew" it was much too hot and too early (the "terrible too's") to rattle up bucks in South Texas during the first days of November. Back then it was also a known fact you could not rattle up whitetails with mule deer antlers. It simply could not happen. In fact, horn rattling also reportedly did not work outside of a few areas in South Texas. Such information appeared in many of our national outdoor publications. Of course today we know better. But even these days we all too often take what we hear or read as gospel and accept information without question. We have become followers, rather than innovators. I for one think it is time we start taking what we hear, read, and sometimes even see with a few grains of salt.

I have been a white-tailed deer enthusiast/deer hunter for nearly four decades and a wildlife biologist involved in white-tailed deer research and management for over half of that time, so I've had lots of opportunity to read widely on white-tailed deer. Over the years I've often gotten tickled over some of the statements made about white-tailed deer and hunting. Hunting is a dynamic sport, and it is ever changing. Witness the advent of the various grunt calls and scents we see on the market today: Frankly speaking, all of us are looking for something that will give us the edge in taking a wily old whitetail or a mossy horn.

Only quite recently have hunters and researchers become aware of how vocal white-tailed deer actually are. While not being quite as "gabby" as elk, they do make a lot of sounds. Quite a few years ago I was involved in a research project where as part of our program we maintained a fairly large herd of captive white-tailed deer. At the time I found it extremely interesting to listen to the vocalizations of the does throughout most of the year, especially between fawning and early fall. Some of the does were extremely vocal, while others vocalized only on rare occasions. Most of the sounds, which included soft grunts, were associated with communication between does and their fawns.

After fawns were weaned and the fall breeding season approached, the does practically quit making sounds completely. The only sound they made was an occasional shrill alarming whistle, a familiar sound most of us have heard while hunting. Even during estrus when a doe's desires were at their highest, they did not utter a sound. During a doe's estrus period, however, she became extremely nervous; when seen being chased by a buck, she would hold her tail at half mast, or essentially straight out rather than held high as when in an alarmed state.

Admittedly, my experience has mostly been with deer herds where there was a relatively narrow buck-to-doe ratio. However in some situations the buck-to-doe ratio was quite wide, with nearly twenty does for every buck. Perhaps in herds where there are nearly as many bucks as does, does have little need to be vocal during the breeding season. On the other hand, if there is only one buck to take care of the needs of twenty does, it would seem does would need to be vocal in order to attract a buck.

The bucks are a completely different story. As the rut or breeding season approaches, bucks become more vocal. During the rest of the year they are relatively quiet. In the same set of pens described earlier, we had two or three mature bucks in the operation at all times. As the rut approached, the bucks grunted more and more. When two bucks confronted each other, separated by a stout wire fence, their challenges to each other began with short "egk-like" guttural grunts. The grunts graduated to what deer behaviorist term the snort-wheeze. This sounds somewhat like a guttural "fit, fit, fit, ffffffeeeeeeeeeeeeeeeeeeeeeeee!" Such a vocalization was followed by antler fighting through the fences.

I have seen the same sequence many times in the wild as well. On those occasions when we separated a doe and induced estrus, the bucks within seeing and smelling distance paced the fence closest to the female and grunted. There was no vocal responses from the does. During the rut the mature bucks walked around their pens, usually about two acres in size, occasionally grunting their soft "egk" sound. They would check does to determine if any were approaching estrus. If one was found, the chase was on. With nearly every step, or at least every four or five steps, the buck grunted a raspy "egk" sound. The doe made no vocalization.

Interestingly back then, when we mentioned the vocalizations to some of the whitetail hunting authorities of the time, we were laughed at. "You deer biologists think you know it all. Everyone knows the only sound deer make is a whistling snort when they are scared or spooked." This statement was always followed by a round of hearty laughter! As mentioned earlier deer hunting is dynamic and ever changing. Times change.

Today we are all looking for the easy way to take a big buck, looking for a "trick," which will give us an added advantage. Never before in history have there been more deer calls, scents, and lures on the market. Someone writes a glowing report about a new deer call and immediately we flock by the thousands to our local sporting goods store. "Boy, I need one of those calls that attracts the dominant buck! All I attracted with the one I used last season was spikes and forkhorns. I want one of those calls that is sure to attract only the eight pointers." When I hear such statements, I often wonder if indeed there are mature or "dominant" bucks where the speaker hunts.

Deer by their own nature are extremely curious, much more so than normally given credit. But deer are also very individualistic in their behavior. This idea is also quite modern. Somewhere in the past the idea that "all deer are produced from the same mold" was created. That is simply not the case, nor is such a statement true. The deer population is comprised of individuals, just the same as is the human population.

On some of the ranches I have managed in the past, I have had the opportunity to "play with the minds of deer." When I placed a foreign object in an area where I frequently saw deer, some approached the object immediately. Others continued to avoid the object even after it had been present for two or more months. Curiosity is one of the reasons some calls and scents work. They do not sound or smell like anything with which the deer have ever before come in contact. But you cannot solely depend on the curiosity of the deer if your aim is to be a consistently successful hunter.

Several years ago articles on "the apple-orchard buck" were ubiquitous—you literally couldn't pick up a deer-hunting magazine without finding a story about bucks and apple orchards. The theme to all these articles revolved around the premise, given as fact, that the only way to take a good buck was to hunt near apple orchards. While apple orchards might be quite common in some parts of the country, that is simply not the case everywhere. It's a fact that some deer may never even have seen an apple.

A friend of mine upon returning from a hunting trip in the Hondo Valley of New Mexico (an area known for abundant and excellent apples) brought back a load of bright red apples, which he dumped on his ranch in southern Texas. "We're gonna test this apple theory," he said. If deer love apples so much, these apples ought to disappear nearly overnight." Three months later the untouched pile of apples was still there. A

A FEW GRAINS OF SALT!

few deer tracks were present around the pile indicating they had come by to check out this new object in their home. But the deer never even took a bite. Why? I think its safe to assume that they did not know what apples were; it's obvious that they didn't know they were supposed to love to eat them.

Do some scents and lures work the same way? To a point I think so. Some companies do their best to use only deer urine, others are less ethical. During the time does are in estrus, they do not urinate a lot, and, when they do, they only release a few drops. Let's think about this last statement, and then let's consider the time a doe is actually in estrus. Allowing a few hours before and after, we are talking about a time period of less than forty-eight hours. Unbred and unsettled, she may come into estrus as many as four to seven times. At the very most, she will not produce a whole lot of urine during her "hot" days. Then consider the great number of products on the market today they contain "pure doe in estrus" urine. It amounts to thousands of gallons! Seems to me we need to use several grains of salt in evaluating this veritable sea of products.

My personal experience with the various scents has spanned several years and involved many, many products. This experience also includes having live deer at my disposal. Some of these scents and lures have worked for me in a fashion, but not with any consistency. Several bucks might walk right past where I have put out a doe-in-heat scent or some other lure and pay no attention to them whatsoever. Then a buck will come by and literally go bonkers over the stuff. Perhaps it is a matter of taste. After all, each deer is an individual. To me it makes little difference whether the "stuff" works or not. What is important is whether the hunter believes it will work. If he truly believes, then he feels confident, and this confidence makes him much more attentive and aware of what is going on around him. That in itself will make him a much better hunter as well as increasing his chances of success.

A few years ago I had several hunters in one of my camps. I divided them into two groups and gave each a container of my "special doe-in-heat deer lure." Unknown to them, one group was given a commercially available deer lure, the other group was given pure distilled water. The containers were the same, new plastic squeeze bottles, marked only "A" and "B."

PEAR FLAT PHILOSOPHIES

At the end of the several-day hunt, I asked for results. According to those hunters, hunting on a well-managed ranch with a buck-to-doe ratio of one buck per one doe, both groups had mixed results. The hunters using distilled water as a lure reported attracting just as many deer as did those using the commercially produced deer lure. Perhaps the deer were curious about why the spot was wet? Interestingly, hunters from both groups were totally convinced that the good bucks they took were because they got to use the "special" deer lure!

My assumption is that they believed the lure would work for them, and as a result they were more attentive and observant while hunting. Incidentally there is now some research being conducted that indicates does do not communicate the state of her estrus cycle through urine. This, just at the time "we thought we knew all there is to know about whitetails!"

Quite often these days we see or hear about a buck's territory. In a recent study conducted in southern Texas, mature white-tailed bucks were radio-collared and tracked for a couple of years; some were tracked even longer. Throughout the period of a year, the researchers found certain bucks roamed over a 10,000-acre area, known as a home range (where deer spend most of their time throughout the period of a year). Others traveled an area only half that figure. Still others were homebodies traveling even smaller home ranges.

The researchers also found some bucks had definite areas where they spent spring and summer. Then as the breeding seasons approached, they moved to another area, only to return to the spring and summer range after the rut. Sounds to me as if each buck had an individual preference. The habitat in this area is fairly similar throughout. Hunting pressure, although present, is extremely light by most standards. Does this mean white-tailed bucks behave similarly throughout the whitetail's range? I doubt it seriously. I strongly suspect there are areas where home ranges are considerably larger, yet in other areas extremely smaller. In such places as the Midwest, I doubt seriously there are 10,000 acres of truly good deer habitat within an area of fifty square miles. Yet those same areas produce some of the largest antlered and largest bodied whitetails in North America.

[166]

A FEW GRAINS OF SALT!

As research becomes increasingly sophisticated, we are learning more and more about rubs and scrapes, both of which are primarily signposts for whitetails. Essentially these signposts simply say to other deer, both bucks and does, "I'm here!" Unlike what some would have us believe, whitetails are not particularly territorial, other than they normally live in a definite area, such as previously described. Earlier I mentioned research being conducted related to does and urine. Those same researchers (from the University of Georgia) suggest rather than using urine from does as a lure, perhaps the best deer lures are those that contain urine from mature bucks. Such lures might make the resident mature bucks think another mature buck has moved into an area and planning on establishing himself. Sounds interesting. . . .

One of the most successful deer hunters in the town where I live is a strong believer in "mock scrapes." However his approach is a bit different from those we read about or even

hear about. When I approached him about his mock scrape technique, he was a bit reluctant to discuss it. At first I thought it was a question of not wanting to divulge his secret. When he finally told me, I understood his reluctance. Juan's secret is very simple: He uses his own human urine to establish mock scrapes. He does not worry about human odors contaminating the scrape. Essentially he locates an active scrape and simply urinates in it every day when he is in the deer pasture. According to him this infuriates the local bucks, which in turn makes them return to the scrape much more often than usual. Perhaps to cover the scent of the last buck to use the scrape? Do I recommend the technique? Not necessarily. But I have learned a long time ago, "Do Not Argue with Success!"

White-tailed bucks make scrapes, that is a fact. But recently we have started seeing and reading a lot about territorial scrapes, boundary scrapes, and even primary scrapes and secondary scrapes. Pass the salt. Quite honestly a scrape is a scrape is a scrape! Bucks make scrapes in the areas where they live, not along their territory, because such territories normally do not exist. Some scrapes are used more than others simply because these scrapes are located in an area where a bucks spends most of his time. This seems reason enough to hunt close to active scrapes. All too often we like to categorize things and try to make them more complicated than they truly are.

There seems to be a misconception that only one buck will visit a particular scrape. This is certainly not the case. Personally I have seen as many as twelve bucks visit a scrape during a six-hour period. Quite possibly other bucks visited the same scrape as well. In this particular instance, five of the bucks visiting that particular scrape were big mature bucks. All worked the licking branch, scraped the ground, urinated in the scrape, then continued on their way. Was one of these a dominant buck and all the rest merely subordinate bucks? There is no sure way of knowing, but I would suspect any of the five big bucks could easily have been THE dominant buck on any particular occasion.

Several years ago a very prominent deer research scientist made a statement about white-tailed deer, which holds true even today, although our research and the techniques at our disposal have become more sophisticated. His statement? "You

A FEW GRAINS OF SALT!

know, there is a whole lot we don't understand about these critters!" The same is true of hunting white-tailed deer: Never close your mind to new techniques and theories, but never take any of them to heart without a good dose of salt!

Marmot Rock

To some of us there is no finer place on this planet than the Rockies during the early fall when aspen leaves turn a brilliant yellow, providing a vivid contrast to the verdure of the pines, spruce, and firs. The shrill bugling of bull elk drifts through the high meadows. The haunting, echoing sound conjures up thoughts of great stags and of loves won and lost. The occasional raucous cawing of the raven, the gibberish of the magpie, and the eerie yapping and yodeling of the coyote accompany the symphony performed by the wind blowing through the needles and boughs of the pines. The first snow-flakes fall silently in the high country. Ahhh . . . fall has returned at last!

But alas, fall cannot forever be. For as is the nature of things, winter and its harshness must follow the fall, and the renewing spring must follow the cold dormancy of winter. With the spring, the bull elk grows silent and contents himself by satiating his hunger on the lush grasses to fortify his body and develop his antlers, while his cows and their offspring suckle gently with the promise of a new generation. The symphony of spring in the Rockies takes on a new melody, if indeed the gobble of the Merriams turkey can be described in such delicate terms.

The lure of the Rockies in the springtime and the promise of a Merriams turkey had brought our band of . . . ah . . . ah. . . . Perhaps it is better at this point if I present the following evidence as prepared by one of my *companeros del cazador.* The names have been changed somewhat to protect the guilty. Me, I tried numerous times to best describe our successful, yet laid-back hunt and failed. Johnnie Hudman, on the other hand, succeeded and sent me the following. I present it here as much for the enjoyment of those who experienced the hunt as for those who were unfortunately absent. Mr. Hudman, if you please. . . .

The Biscuit Queen and Mr. Crazy were sitting amongst the remnants of the previous nights' campfire meeting. Empty containers previously containing vast and copious amounts of knowledge, invincibility, and bullet-proofness were neatly stacked against a nearby pine. The current discussion centered around the upcoming afternoon's turkey hunt. Mr. Crazy had already taken his bird and so felt obligated to impart his vast turkey-hunting knowledge along with various pointers and tips to the Queen so she too might take a gobbler. Mr. Crazy felt assured she needed some help, especially since the local Merriams turkey population scattered throughout this land of rocks, canyons, junipers, and pines had contacted a serious case of lockjaw, compliments of the reoccurring cold weather. Even an early morning gobble from a roost tree was a rarity. Mr. Crazy was about to put the finishing touches on some expert advice when the Queen pointed toward the nearby creek bottom and said:

"Look, a rabbit!"

"Looks more like a marmot to me," argued Mr. Crazy.

"That's no marmot!" answered the Queen.

"It is too!" insisted Mr. Crazy.

Having had several arguments with the Biscuit Queen in the past, Mr. Crazy knew the futility of pursuing the debate, so he discontinued his stance. Royalty always demanded the last word.

As they walked to the area where the phantom had disappeared, Double L, noted for giving good fires and smoke, came over to see what the ruckus was all about. Upon hearing all the facts in the case, he deliberated for a moment and then stated that, in all likelihood, the elevation was too high for the phantom to have been a marmot. Thus informed, the small group continued toward the creek.

When they arrived, the phantom had vanished, like the contents of the bottle of knowledge and wisdom the night before. Mr. Crazy started to mention that perhaps the mystical critter had been a ferret, but then he recalled that almost all the ferrets had been exported to England to be used in the sport of trouser stuffing.

MARMOT ROCK

Along the creek's bank was a huge rock with a long, flat area on top. A few small pines blocked out some sunshine, but most of the flat rock's surface had been warmed by early afternoon sun. The Biscuit Queen announced she believed this was an ideal place for a rabbit's den. Mr. Crazy retorted it looked much more like a good place for a marmot's den. Double L proclaimed it unsuitable for either but stated it looked like a perfect place to take a nap. After a brief discussion, the Biscuit Queen and Mr. Crazy agreed, but the nap would have to wait until the morrow, as time grew near for the afternoon's hunt.

The next day proved to be another breathtakingly beautiful, yet cool, day. After a hard morning's hunt, followed by steaks and pies of cherries and berries from the Bear Claw's kitchen, a nap seemed to be in order. Mr. Crazy told the Biscuit Queen that he intended to journey to Marmot Rock to take a nap. To his total amazement, she agreed and went to fetch a much-overstuffed pillow. On the way to the napping spot, they ran into Double L and shared the thought with him. He too agreed with the idea and stated he would be there momentarily.

The Queen and Mr. Crazy proceeded to the rock, and each found a comfortable spot to stretch out. Anticipation was high for a snooze in the sunshine. Just as the Queen closed her eyes, Mr. Crazy asked, "Have I ever told you about the time. . . ." Just as he finished his tale, Double L arrived. As he stretched his long frame comfortably on the warm stone, he said to the other two, "Did I ever tell you about the time I. . . ."

As story followed story, it was obvious that Mr. Crazy's could have been true, but one had to wonder about those told by the Queen and Double L. Just as all eyes closed, up walked Well-rope Cowboy, who is in turn scribe, sage, soothsayer, connoisseur of old western movies, the Queen's roommate, and a pretty damned good musician with a diaphragm turkey call. He too agreed that the flat sun-warmed stone was a fine napping rock.

Eyelids grew heavy, and it seemed peace was settling upon the foursome when Double L said, "Did I ever tell ya'll about the time. . . ." Conversation again took the place of a restful nap. Once the tale was completed, all eyes closed for a final. . . . The silence was once again shattered when the Queen began, "Did I ever tell ya'll . . . Oh! Look! There's a zillion spiders over here!"

[173]

PEAR FLAT PHILOSOPHIES

The Well-rope Cowboy got up and ambled over to where the Biscuit Queen was lounging. You see, Well-rope has traveled over a goodly portion of the world, but he had never seen a zillion spiders gathered in a single place, so he wanted to take a look. But by the time he had walked the ten feet that separated his spot from that of the Biscuit Queen's, some 999 crillion, 999 trillion, 999 billion, 999 million, 999 thousand, and 998 spiders had vanished! As the Biscuit Queen stared intently at the base of the rock, the Well-rope Cowboy counted two. One has to wonder how that vast number of spiders could so quickly disappear!

"Are you sure there were a full zillion?" asked the Well-rope Cowboy as he shoved back his hat in wonderment.

"I seeeeen um!" snapped the Queen.

Without further comment, the Well-rope Cowboy retreated to his napping spot. He also knew it did no good to argue with Royalty.

With the intense excitement of the disappearing spiders behind them, the group again attempted to nap. But alas, either the stimulating intellectual conversation or the extreme excitement of the vanishing spiders proved too much for the group to sleep. So it only seemed appropriate when Double L said, "Did I ever tell you about the time. . . ."

After that story, everyone gave up on the idea of a nap, got up and made their way to the campfire. After kicking at the remaining coals and melting the soles of his boots, the Well-rope Cowboy showed the group his rendition of the around the campfire popular, the 'hotfoot/softshoe.' But when the group called for an encore, he appropriately announced, "Let's go hunting before I burn up anymore of my boots!" So everyone readied themselves for the evening hunt.

They never did see the mystery animal again. As to who finally won the argument, Mr. Crazy smiled as he left for his evening hunt. The Biscuit Queen had, with a slip of the tongue, referred to the napping area as 'Marmot Rock,' as the foursome made plans for the morrow.

Well, with all that settled, I'll bet you think it's time for a little nap. "Did I ever tell you about the time I. . . ."

Mountain Climbing and Boot Burning

"Any tale is far better for the telling by a campfire!"

The night before there had been quite a few tales told around our campfire. As the evening progressed, there were even several tales that should have come under the category of sworn-to-secrecy and under-oath-happenings, and I think the details should best go unmentioned here. I was quite satisfied: It appeared this would be another of those camps where it would not take long to spend the night, at least not when it came to sleeping. Long before daylight, our host opened the flap to my tent, lit a Coleman lantern, set it next to my cot, and shoved a hot cup of cowboy coffee into my hand. From the old log cabin, which served as a kitchen/dining room, came the delicious aroma of freshly baked sourdough biscuits, intertwined with bacon being fried in a black cast-iron skillet. I know of no, non-living innovations, that can stir me to rise out of bed more quickly.

Upon entering the old cabin, I saw a twinkle in the Irishman's eyes. Immediately, I should have known he had something up his sleeve other than his long red underwear. "Have I got a turkey spot picked out for you and Fears to hunt this morning! It's tailor made for ya'll. We found it yesterday, just before dark when we watched several gobblers go to roost. As soon as you eat, let's hit the trail. It's a pretty long drive from here to where we're hunting this morning, and we need to get you and Wayne in position before first light."

The drive to our hunting area from base camp took over thirty minutes. Even so, by the time we got to the appointed jump-off point, there was still not so much as a hint of predawn pink in the eastern sky.

PEAR FLAT PHILOSOPHIES

"What you two guys need to do is to make your way up the slope on the left. It shouldn't be much of a walk for the two of you, experienced as you are. Yesterday the gobbler flew to the top of the flat-top ridge just up the slope there. Better get on your way, so you'll be in position before daylight," said our outfitter.

Wayne and I gathered up our gear, grabbed a couple of flashlights, and started making our way up the slope. The lower part was not all that tough, other than the buckbrush was so thick that it was almost impenetrable. Just about the time we had snaked our way through about a hundred yards of tangle, the batteries in our flashlights started playing out. To save them for an emergency, we turned them off. The night was inky black. Yet we continued on, sort of feeling our way farther up the slope, which now became rocky and considerably steeper. From walking upright, we had to start crawling hand over hand, slowly and carefully working our way up the rugged slope. What had started out as a supposedly leisurely stroll was beginning to become serious work, nay, dangerous work! Upward we continued in the dark, literally feeling our way along.

Several times we used our flashlights long enough to determine we were about to step into nothingness, at which point we retreated as far as we could and planned another approach. By now perspiration had soaked our camouflage clothing, even though the morning was cold. We took advantage of any and every hand-hold and crevice in the rocks until we reached a level where we could not turn around or retreat. We had no choice but to continue upward and forward as best we could. Ropes and repelling equipment would have been much more appropriate for the situation, and certainly far more helpful. The fun had long since flown the coop for this morning.

At one point my companion turned to me and said, "Are we really doing this for turkeys? Are we crazy or what? I've not had to climb in this kind of country since the last time I hunted bighorn sheep. And, I don't remember it being this tough! If we could, we ought to turn around and go back down into the canyon. If we could. . . ." I nodded in agreement.

The climbing had now become torturous. We felt more like stranded mountain climbers rather than turkey hunters. Finally it had gotten light enough to see our predicament. We were not inexperienced outdoorsmen, and we were scared! Under no circumstances would we have undertaken the climb had we seen what lay ahead of us in daylight. We would have gladly turned around if that had been an option, yet the possibility of a rock slide now prevented any retreating. The slope ahead ranged from perpendicular to a reverse overhang. Wayne and I took turns playing human flies. The only thing that kept us going was devising pleasurable tortures that we could inflict on the Irishman. Plans ranged from setting him afloat in a cottonmouth moccasin- and alligator-infested swamp, to using him as grizzly bait in Canada. Revenge is sweet.

The last few feet were the toughest, but finally we pulled ourselves to the top of the mesa. For several minutes we simply stood there, breathing heavily, thankful we had finally reached the top and the climb had been completed. It was then we saw a road that lead to within mere feet of where we now stood, albeit a more circuitous route, through the bottom of the canyon. To make matters worse after our already long "challenging" climb, we watched the gobblers, which we had been told would fly up on top where we were, fly right to the bottom of the broad canyon. A few moments later, we heard the sound of a shotgun being fired. At that point we realized we had served simply as decoys or blockers to keep the turkeys from going up on top. The Irishman had done it to us again!

Seeing the route we had taken, aided by full daylight, made our knees wobble. Had we not started under the cover of darkness, there is no way we would have ever attempted the climb, shy of knowing a monstrous mule deer buck lived on top. Even at that, it would have been questionable lunacy. Regardless of whatever treachery we could devise for the Irishman, none seemed equal to what he deserved.

After looking around a bit, I found a way to get back to the canyon's floor without any difficulty. Once there, we confronted the Irishman. He started laughing. "I can't believe you two guys crawled up that bluff. I doubt a Rocky Mountain goat could have made that climb. But you'll have to admit my plan worked." He then continued, "Honestly, I never really dreamed you would take me seriously about making that climb. . . ."

PEAR FLAT PHILOSOPHIES

My compadre and I looked at each other and smiled . . . some day revenge would be sweet.

That night there would be talk around the campfire of tall peaks, mountain goats, the pitfalls of turkey hunting, and past camp fires. A couple of seasons earlier, while hunting with the Irishman, I had fallen asleep with my boot-ed feet resting on rocks next to the fire. I was awakened by the smell of burning rubber and by an extra-warm sensation on the soles of my feet. After hopping around for a while, I finally got the fire on the bottom of my boots put out. The Irishman laughed so hard that I thought he'd fall on the ground and break a leg. I, however, did not see the humor in the situation . . . well, at least not as much as he did!

Later that day as evening turned to night, I started carrying firewood to the camp's fire pit. Tonight we would have a campfire that would be the best of the hunt. That night's evening meal was truly a feast. The hearty meal of roastlike steaks was finished off with cherry cobbler, baked in a cast-iron Dutch oven. It did not take long for the other hunters and our host to "gravitate" toward "my" campfire.

Tale after tale was regaled. Laughter drifted through the canyon. As the night grew colder, I got a little closer to the fire and propped my feet on the rock that formed the fire pit. A short time later the rubber on the bottom of my boots started smoldering, then smoking. The Irishman hooted with laughter and rolled on the ground, poking fun at the guy from Texas who wore a big hat and burned the soles right off of his boots. He laughed and laughed. I smiled, seeing more humor in the moment than the Irishman realized. . . .

Later that night, after everyone had gone to sleep I slipped into the Irishman's tent and "returned" his hunting boots that I had "borrowed" to wear "around" the campfire that night. . . .

The Elder Statesman

The old gobbler stared down from his perch high in the boughs of the ancient oak. All around him, the world was gray, gray as the uniforms of the Confederate soldiers who had once marched along the spring-fed creek with the intention of protecting it with their very lives.

The early spring sun would soon arrive, illuminating the old bird's domain and sharing its warmth with all the creatures of the creek bottom—of which the old gobbler was undisputed king. Younger, foolish gobblers had tried to dethrone him, but his adeptness at using both wings and spurs allowed him to quickly subdue all his rivals, sending them speedily on their way. Those that fell in conflict with the king never questioned his authority again. He bore the scars of several such encounters. The coolness of this particular morning made those old injuries ache more than usual.

Off in the distance a coyote yapped an early morning greeting. The soloist was soon joined by others in the small family group, creating a symphony appreciated by only a few of those who lived in the creek bottom. He knew the coyotes well, several times he had eluded their grasp. Once he nearly lost it all, barely escaping by a tail feather. He had been showing off to a young hen and had become so engrossed with her that he had failed to notice the old male coyote creep to within mere inches of his fanned out backside.

Suddenly there had been a blur of movement, coming right at him. The old gobbler saw the blurring motion in time to spring forward and start flapping his wings to escape. As his feet left the ground, the coyote's teeth grasped a tail feather tightly. Fear spread through his body, like the cold, chilling winds of January. He flapped his wings harder, pulling at the air to become airborne. Just when it seemed he would become a coyote's meal, the feather jerked loose from his tail. He propelled forward. There was a slight pain, but a pain he thankfully accepted as he flew free of the grasp of the coyote. The old coyote would have waited a while longer before he dined on wild turkey, especially this wild turkey!

No sooner had the coyote's symphony trailed off, echoing as it drifted off the bluff a little farther down the creek, than the old gobbler let out a mighty response of his own, just to remind the world he was still there.

Gobbbbbllle,obble,obbble,obble. . . . He listened as his gobbling echoed through the still morning.

Way off in the distance, well beyond where the coyotes had serenaded, came the gobble of another turkey. It was unfamiliar to the old gobbler and sounded vaguely like a challenge! The old gobbler let forth several more thunderous gobbles. He did not fully understand or comprehend why. It simply seemed like the thing to do. Perhaps, he was proclaiming he was happy with his position in life. Perhaps he simply wanted to impress the hens with a bit of vocalization before showing off his finest new feathers, for later he planned to strut for them. Perhaps it was just to spite the interloper.

From off in the distance came the annoying gobbling of the stranger, almost as if he was mocking him. He pretended he did not hear it. But, deep down he knew that some day, the day would come when he would be challenged, just as he had challenged and then defeated the boss gobbler before him.

Dawn's early gray light brought with it myriad sounds. The old gobbler, still perched high in his roost tree, listened as small birds greeted the morning with their own songs and medleys. From down below, he heard what he thought was the yelp of a young hen. He turned quickly to stare in the direction of the sound. A mockingbird flitted to another limb and seemed to laugh at the old gobbler. He stared hard in the smaller bird's direction. It was bad enough that he might be challenged by another gobbler before the day was over, but he really did not need the annoyance of some little smart-aleck bird giving him a hard time; to have the coyotes taunting him, with their awful yapping, would be the final straw!

THE ELDER STATESMAN

Off in the distance came the challenging gobble of the stranger. The old bird became more and more irritated. He responded with the best of his gobbles, trying to sound superior, aggressive, and dangerous to any other gobbler daring to enter his domain and challenge the boss. Full daylight had come quicker than the old gobbler realized or remembered. He was still in the tree long after several hens had flown to the ground and started their daily routine of scratching and looking for tidbits of tasty morsels. He readied himself for the day, shaking vigorously to allow each feather to fall into place.

Off in the distance, although considerably closer than before, came the gobble of the now obvious challenger. He sounded mature, yet, a bit full of his own importance. There had been others who had challenged the boss gobbler, and they had been handily defeated. This one would be no different. He reared back and issued forth a gobble, definitely challenging the intruder. With that he again shook himself and set his wings to fly to the ground. Gliding downward, he hit the ground a bit faster than he intended. He tried desperately to recover, but ended up tumbling end over end. Hurriedly, he jumped up, shook the leaves and litter from his feathers, looked around to be sure no hens or young gobblers were watching, then pretended he had done the full body roll just to impress the ladies. So far, this had not been a particularly good morning.

From not far off in the distance came a thunderous gobble, nearly shaking the leaves off the trees. The old gobbler outwardly pretended not to hear or pay attention to the challenge. Inside he grew more and more irritated. But then, that passed and he started to mentally prepare himself to do battle with the stranger. The challenger kept gobbling. This time less than a hundred yards away. The old gobbler remained quiet and listened.

Just then he heard the seductive yelp of a young hen. Momentarily the challenger was forgotten. The old gobbler came to full strut and started drumming, doing his best to impress the young hen, which could only be a few yards away. When she remained where she was, he gobbled but remained where he was. Almost immediately the stranger responded, but this time the stranger was much closer and obviously making a move toward the hen. Irritated, the old gobbler again gobbled. Immediately the hen responded with a yelp and purr. The challenging gobbler sounded much closer. The old gobbler remained where he was, performing his best strut, stopping only occasionally to gobble, then stretch his neck in the direction of the hen to try to spot her or hear if she might possibly be coming toward him.

Again the challenger gobbled, this time obviously even closer to the old king and to the hen. The old gobbler grew irritated at himself for letting the challenger get to the hen before he did. If only he had not been so careful, he might now be enjoying the company of a young hen. Just as he was about to throw caution to the wind, the challenger gobbled again.

Suddenly a shot sounded and echoed through the creek bottom. For a few moments all was silent. Then. . . .

"Good shot, son! Look at the length of that beard!"

"Yeah Dad, and look at how long his spurs are. They look like sabers! Dad, you sure did a good job of sounding like a hen, you really had that old boss bird fooled. Turkey hunting is great! Thanks for taking me," spoke the higher-pitched voice of the two humans.

"Looks like we're going to have roast wild turkey for dinner next Sunday after all. Let's get back to town so we can show him to your mom."

The old boss bird did not gobble for several minutes, waiting until the sound of the two human's voices had faded away. Somewhere off in the distance the coyotes started yapping. He had never heard a more beautiful sound!